DIVINE INTERVENTION

HOW GOD SAVED ME THROUGH DREAMS

DIVINE INTERVENTION

How God Saved Me Through Dreams

MAUNG MAUNG KYAW ZAW HEIN

Divine Intervention: How God Saved Me Through Dreams
by Maung Maung Kyaw Zaw Hein
Copyright © 2018 by Maung Maung Kyaw Zaw Hein
All Rights Reserved.
ISBN: 978-1-59755-491-6
Published by: **ADVANTAGE BOOKS™**
Longwood, Florida, USA

Library of Congress Catalog Number: 2018968558
1.   REL012000 Religion: Christian Life - Inspirational

First Printing: December 2018
18 19 20 21 22 23 24   10 9 8 7 6 5 4 3 2 1
Printed in the United States of America

To my amazing parents, my sister, friends and everyone else who had been with me throughout my life, I will never be express how grateful I am to have all of you supporting me throughout writing this book. May God richly bless you all in every areas of your life.

May you all know more of his unfailing love in this book!

Table of Contents

About Me!

Dear reader,

Firstly, let me, please tell you a little information about myself. I'm just a very ordinary person who grew up in a Buddhist family in Myanmar, knowing nothing about Christianity or the Bible. There's only one thing in my life that I want to share with you so far and that's this book. This book is mainly about the dreams that God gave me to let me have an assurance that dreams do have meanings and how he saved me through my dreams when I was an atheist before.

Throughout this book, I will tell you all about how God used dreams to change my life for good and have a relationship with Jesus Christ. If you're an atheist and believe that there aren't any supernatural forces around us, I only ask that you keep an open mind while reading this book.

When I was a pre-teen, I only used to believe in good and bad karma. This was the thought I had.

"Do good, and good things will happen to me. Do bad things and bad things will happen to me. I will do good things. If there is an exam, I will study hard and get good results by only my efforts. So why do I need God? "

That was my belief before I became a Christian and it may-be the same belief that you have right now too. However, after you've read this book, you'll understand why I finally trusted in God.

I don't claim to know everything. However, everyone has an area in which he or she has more knowledge of, just as a seven years old kid would know more about cartoons than his 40 years old dad who's a doctor. I have spent so much time studying about what you are about to read in this book. I hope you'll be open to new knowledge and enjoy reading about my experiences with God! May this book convince you to know more about God!

God Bless!

Maung

Chapter 1

How I Got Saved

The First Dream

In 2011, my family and I went on a trip to Malaysia during the summer holidays. During one night of the trip, I dreamt of my own face on my elder sister's chest, and she was hugging me in the dream. When I woke up that morning, I was puzzled about why I even had that dream since my sister, and I were always fighting every day all the time. I thought it only had to be my mind playing tricks in the dream.

When I woke up, I was very interested in the dream that I had. So I searched on the internet about the meaning of the dream, and it said that my sister would help me a lot in my life. I did not believe it at all because we were always against each other and never really had peace with each other.

During the afternoon, we went to the amusement park with our cousins and friends our age. It was all so fun, exciting and frightening at the same time because of the scary twisted roller coaster rides that we had. However, during the evening while walking around there, we found penguins! I was so amazed as it was my first time seeing penguins as an 11 years old. So I immediately put down my bag, opened it and searched for my Ipad to take pictures, and to my horror, it wasn't there in the bag!. I panicked and asked everyone in the group to help me find it, but nobody could find it within themselves or anywhere around. Everyone's reactions were like "We can't find it anywhere. I'm so sorry that you lost your Ipad! You're never getting it back now. Forget it. You have lost it." Everyone's reactions were like that except for my sister (very surprisingly) who was so determined to get my Ipad back for me. We went everywhere around the park thinking that I had accidentally left or dropped my Ipad somewhere but we still couldn't find it anywhere.

When I already gave up the hopes of finding my lost Ipad back, my sister insisted that we go to the main office of the amusement park and ask the staff to let us watch the CCTV footages of us. Unfortunately, the people there refused to show us the CCTV footages due to security concerns. However, then, my sister got mad at them and threatened to call the police if they didn't show us the CCTV footages.

Very surprisingly, they still refused to show it to us, but a staff member went to the other room and appeared to us with an Ipad which happened to be mine! I was so happy to get it back. It was as if I got back the missing half of my heart.

This wouldn't have been possible, and I would have to go back home very upset without my Ipad if my sister wasn't there to help me. During that night while thinking everything over, I realized shockingly that the dream meaning of my dream was proven true to me right on that day.

You may think it was just a coincidence to have a dream the night before and the dreams meaning coming true on that day. However, the chances of me having a dream of my sister comforting me. My sister whom I was always against and fought with, and her helping me so determinedly the next day. The chances of it happening were 100% unbelievable.

This was when I started taking care of my dreams almost every night.

Dreams Do Have Meanings

This happened sometime (around a year) after I had the dream of my sister in Malaysia. In my head, I knew that dreams had meanings, but I wasn't sure of it and didn't care much about it.

I was in primary school that time around Grade 4 or 5 and as a typical boy; I had a crush on a beautiful girl called Ariel (fake name for privacy) in my class at school. I had a friend called Beatrice (fake name for privacy) who was a friend of hers. Beatrice and I were good friends. I had a crush on Ariel but didn't do anything about it. Beatrice knew about it.

Then one night, I had a dream that my face was in front of Beatrice's chest and she was hugging me (the same dream that I had of my sister). The next day, Beatrice told Ariel that I had a crush on her even though I told her to keep it a secret about it. However, Ariel liked me too, and we were in a relationship together for a week (childish). It was a good experience for me to know more about true love in relationships.

In the end, I realized that Beatrice helped me and the dream meaning came true again immediately. It was when I knew that dreams meanings are true.

First God-related Dream

Now I've had some more dreams that helped me or showed me signs of what was going to happen to me in the future, but my journey with God started with this one particular dream that I had when I was around 14 or 15 years old.

During those years, I did not care about God and depended only on my own strength and works for the future. It was just a typical day for me that day. Nothing unusual happened at night before sleeping. So when I was asleep that night, I had a dream where I was in a small room with very red and brown walls. It felt a bit hot in the room which was also very dimly lit but enough to see the whole small room. The room was only about 5 feet long and 6/7 feet tall. I remember I was sitting on a bench alone all by myself in that room. The only strange thing was to unexpectedly hear a voice like that of an angel (which I thought it was at first, but it was the voice of the Holy Spirit) whispering very clearly but softly into my ear. It said this slowly, clearly but softly:

" Do..not...deny...God. There..are..those...who..denied..God"

After hearing those words, suddenly I saw fire/flames in front of me. Then I was shocked and confused about why I would need to know about God.

It was so very detailed, direct and precise. It did not even say "Don't." It said, "Do not." Didn't say "some people denied god" but it said, "there are those who denied God." It was so clear.

During that time, I didn't know anything about God, Jesus, the Holy Spirit or the Bible. I still ignored it for some years and only in 2017, I started to get to know about Christianity and was bewildered by what I discovered. There were verses that supported my dream.

- Job 33 says God gives men dreams and visions to save himself from hell

- Matthew 25:16 *"Then they will go away to eternal punishment, but the righteous to eternal life."*

- Revelation 21:8 *"But the cowardly, the unbelieving, the vile, the murderers, the sexually immoral, those who practice magic arts, the idolaters and all liars—they will be consigned to the fiery lake of burning sulfur. This is the second death."*

Even one lie can send a person to Hell in Christianity

After knowing much more about Christianity, I understood that we are all full of sins and how much good deeds we do in our lives can never erase our past sins. God is a just judge and loves humans so much. The problem was that every sin has to be punished. However, God cannot compromise his righteousness by freely forgiving humans at no cost.

Why is there evil in the world? It's because our world is a fallen world (and it's only going to get worse). People need to understand that God gave the whole Earth to Man at first and God does not take it back if Man did anything bad against him. When God gives, God gives it freely. He doesn't say "you did this against me? OK, now give it back to me."

However, Man gave control of the Earth to the devil since the moment Adam sinned against God. So all of Adam's seed, including you and I, are born of sin-nature. That's why Jesus had to be born of a virgin.

So God had to send his son, Jesus Christ into the world to live a life without any sins and to die on the cross in exchange for his perfect life for all our sins, past, present and future so that whoever believes in Jesus as their lord and savior would be saved. That is once again, a gift from God for all of our sins.

The Earth was a perfect and peaceful place before the fall (sin of Adam). All the animals and living things lived together in peace on the Earth. No animals ate each other, and the world was not competitive, it was just like heaven. However, when Adam sinned, the Bible said the world became 'cursed,' and the ground grew thorns (showing that the world became competitive, animals started fighting against each other for survival). This is because when the highest of all God's creation, Adam, sinned, all the rest of the creation along with Adam became a curse. That's when death entered into the world.

This is why Jesus also wore the "crown of thorns" on the cross. He lived a perfect life without sin (only he was capable of it as he was God in the flesh), took away the curse of the world along with him on the cross when the divine exchange took place; our sins for his righteousness and his righteousness for our sins as he hung and died on the cross.

In Christianity, people who denied Jesus cannot go to heaven because heaven is a perfect place and sin cannot be allowed in heaven. So these sinful people have only one place to go after they die, which is hell. Hell is so much worse than you can ever imagine.

Hell is dark because God is light (1 John 1:7)

There's only death in hell because God is life (1 John 1:4)

There's only hatred in hell because God is love (John 4:15)

There's no mercy in hell because the mercy of the lord is in the heavens (Psalms 36:5)

There's no strength in hell because the Lord gives us strength (Psalms 18:32).

There's no water in hell because water is the rain of heaven (Deuteronomy 11:11)

There's no peace in hell because he is the prince of peace (Isaiah 1:6)

The earth is full of the goodness of the lord (Psalms 33:5)

Deny God and all the good things go together with him, and there's a place (which is hell) that has nothing to do with him other than his wrath that is poured out as a form of fire because God hates sins.

I believe that's also why Lucifer (Satan) became evil the moment he turned away from God and became all the opposite of God's good qualities

When I thought about that warning dream, it was very convincing, but I always thought I had that dream due to my mind playing tricks and happened by chance.

However, very faithfully, God gave me another dream the following night which was just another evidence that I needed to be convinced. I believed that having dreams previously that came true were just for me to be already convinced that dreams are important so that when God would give me dreams to come to him, I would be convinced. Also, God just gave me that warning dream just at the right time for me to be serious about it.

Evidence That Was Needed

The next following night, I had another dream where I was in outer space. Everything was black with tiny lights. Then I saw two giant hands, the size of a planet, holding up a planet and showing it to me. Somehow I knew that the planet's name was "Bary 2". It was like something just put the information in my head about the planet's name.

I did not understand at all why I had that dream until two years later when I searched about it in the Bible. It was a proof that God gave me to let me convince that he is real.

I found this Bible verse

Psalms 147:4 (NLT) "He counts the stars and calls them all by name."

I only found out about those verses after I became a Christian and was incredibly astonished by it. Sometimes, I think I got those dreams because I used to listen to rock music a lot when those songs turned out to be Christian rock songs. I'm not sure, but I think I got those dreams also because when I was a baby, I had a Hirschsprung disease. I had an operation to remove my large intestine after the 1st day of birth and spent most of the time in the hospital. During those times, all of my caretakers inside the hospital were Christians (even though almost all Burmese people were Buddhist at that time). They prayed for me and played Christian songs around me for me all the time. It was also amazing because my parents told me that when my sister was in the hospital after birth, all her caretakers were Buddhist but only for me, all my caretakers were Christians.

Psalms 139:13 "For you created my inmost being; you knit me together in my mother's womb."

Sometimes, I think God allowed this Hirsch-sprung disease for me so that the Christian caretakers at the hospital could pray for me and I think that's why I have these dreams.

First Dream after Becoming a Christian

I know that we all want to know what our future holds for us. What will our future wife/husband look like? Is he/she of our preference? What job will we have? What will our lives look like 20 years from now? As a teenager, I was very obsessed about knowing those things and also being a chess player traveling around the world to play in chess tournaments with the Myanmar chess team. I always wondered if I would be successful in chess in the future or if my future wife would be a patient and beautiful chess player. The closest an unbeliever person can come to these answers is by talking to a fortune teller (which God doesn't like, by the way). However, I didn't know anything about the Bible or Jesus that time and so here's my story which I am sure you can relate to.

During April 2017, I went on a short trip to Melbourne, Australia. My family and I had breakfast at a Japanese restaurant one morning. As I was very picky about food, I asked my parents to allow me to have breakfast at KFC across the street alone instead of having breakfast with them (which they allowed).

Along my way, I met a fortune teller on the street who walked up to me and said I would become so rich or successful in July. As he was very friendly and all, I offered him to have breakfast together with me in KFC to continue our chat. After we ordered food, went upstairs and sat down, he told me everything about himself. Then he had me write down my future dreams and my basic details such as how many siblings I have, etc. He went to the toilet while I was doing that and when he came back, I had the paper hidden in my hand, and without me telling him anything, he wrote down exactly everything on another piece of paper which I just wrote in the paper squeezed and hidden in my hand. That was how he proved that he had some supernatural powers and that completely amazed me as a teenager. So I was asking him so many questions out of great curiosity about what my future holds for me as we all would ask if we had the chance. I was desperate to know the answers to everything as I didn't know what I was doing in life as I was going through it aimlessly and just wanted something positive to hope in and keep on going. Unfortunately, while he was just about to answer my questions, my whole family came up and out of worry, told me to leave him because they didn't trust him.

After the incident, I felt so hollow and sad in my heart as if I missed the only chance to know the biggest questions of my life. I blamed my family as a typical teenager would and was very extremely sad that I was in a significant depression and ended up crying that night alone. All because I had nothing to hope in for my future and I didn't see the point of going through life without any hope or a promise in the future.

However, I remembered that the fortune teller told me that I would be very successful in July and I had a big chess tournament in July. I believed I would win that tournament, but I got sick in the middle of the two weeks long tournament and lost so miserably. I declared to myself not to believe in any fortune telling stuff anymore and just assumed his fortune telling was wrong. However, very surprisingly and unexpectedly, I became a Christian on 28th July 2017! After stumbling upon a YouTube video about hell, realizing that the Bible verses mentioned in the video related to the dreams I had. I also discovered how much God loves us and it touched my heart. It was the best thing that has ever happened to me so far.

When I said the prayers and accepted Jesus into my heart alone in my room, I could feel the energy throughout my whole body and even to the bones from the top of my head to my toes. It was an experience that I had never felt before in my life. It was like in a cartoon where an ugly beast goes up into the air, shined so brightly and magically transformed into a handsome prince. It was just like that but from the insides.

My whole life changed as if my eyes have finally been opened to the truth and the meaning of life. Honestly speaking, I was a Buddhist/kind of like an atheist before that time as all my family and friends were Buddhist and I just thought to myself "I will have this amazing relationship with Jesus and be saved from hell and still be a Buddhist, there's only gains for me! What a smart move. If it is free, just take it, and Jesus is a free gift for me by God, so I will take." Only days later, I became a full Christian after discovering more about the amazing grace and love of God for us.

Then one day, I started to think about all the bad things I've done in life and wasn't sure if God forgave me of all my horrible sins in the past. I was feeling very terrible and guilty about it.

One night later, I got a very interesting dream of myself being a thin a4 paper. This thin paper was black, so dirty and had black spots all over it. Suddenly, it started tearing itself from top to bottom in half, and my consciousness was left on one half of the torn paper. I saw myself (half torn paper) as being all so pure and white. Then I saw the other half in front of me. It was so black, had more ugly black spots and looked even dirtier than before. As I was looking at the filthy paper in front of me, I heard a voice from behind me saying very gently,

"Son, you're not that anymore."

I only understood this dream sometime later. At first, I was full of sins, but when I accepted Jesus, I became pure and perfect without any sin anymore. The black dirt and spots represented all of my sins. I'm now the righteousness of God in Christ. God is so good and caring.

I think this verse supports the dream that I had.

John 3:3 (ESV) "Jesus answered him 'Truly I tell you, no one can see the Kingdom of God unless they are born again'"

God showed me in this dream of my old self-dying and being born again as pure and white.

I have always wondered why I have never seen the speaker in my dream as I've heard the voices in some of my dreams. I was astonished and happy when I found this verse from the Bible.

Numbers 12:6 (KJV) "And he said, Hear now my words: If there be a prophet among you, I the LORD will make myself known unto him in a vision, and will speak unto him in a dream."

Only in a vision can a Christian see God but only in a dream can a Christian hear the voice of God. I was like "wow! That explains everything." Well, almost everything.

Chapter 2

Experiencing God's Guidance

Prayer Is Indeed Effective

Some weeks after I became a Christian, I began praying every morning after I woke up and before going to bed at night even though I did not know much about God. One morning, I woke up later than my alarm set time and was late for the IELTS exam. So I did my morning routine very quickly, rushing everything. When I was about to leave home, I suddenly remembered that I had forgotten to pray. I was already at the door, about to leave and was thinking what to do. I was also really shy to pray in front of other people in the house, and so I went back into my room, and I prayed quickly for about 30 secs – 1 min. Then when I left my apartment and was in front of the lift, I saw the elevator being on the 3rd floor (the floor that I live at). When I was about to click the lift button to open the lift doors, the electricity went out suddenly, and the lift also didn't function anymore.

I immediately said, "Oh thank you, Lord!" If I hadn't prayed for 30 seconds and left my apartment, I would surely have gotten inside the lift and get trapped inside for a long time, making me absent from the important exam. It was crucial as I needed the result of that exam to apply for colleges or universities abroad.

You may think I was just lucky, but when we make time to pray, the Holy Spirit guides us to be at the right place at the right time to avoid any kind of danger possible.

Dream of "5:12"

During around late August 2017, I had a dream where I was in the sky with clouds around me as if I were in heaven. Then I saw the numbers "5:12" in front of my eyes in the clouds, and I woke up.

I thought that was just a Bible verse that God wanted to show me but there was no word besides the numbers for a Bible verse. For months, I thought it was an important Bible verse and asked God to help me remember the word, but I got nothing.

I got accepted by Trinity College in September and found out that I had to leave Myanmar in December as my college course was going to start in January. I haven't seen all my good friends from high school since our IGCSE exam in May.

As I saw the numbers "5:12" in the sky and know that all good things come from above. I knew it represented something good, but I wasn't just sure what it was. I later found out that I was going to Australia on 6th December.

I proposed a farewell dinner with all my awesome high school friends on 4th December but had to move it to 5th December due to some circumstances. I only then understood that 5:12 was actually a date and not a Bible verse! I also didn't organize the dinner because of the numbers that I dreamt. In fact, I only remembered that the date and the numbers are the same after I had organized it. 5 / 12/ 2017 was a day full of joy and happiness with all my beloved friends. It was surely a day from above.

I had that dream in August, and it only became true in December. How very fascinating!

Chapter 3

Miracles of Tithing

Nowadays, almost everyone thinks that only stupid people give tithing to church and that the Church is tricking them into giving their money to churches for nothing. However, this is not true at all. Everything we have in life is because of God, and so, we honor God by giving him 10% of the 100% that he has given us. He even gave promises about tithing. Here's a verse about the promise of tithing.

> *Malachi 3:10 "Bring the whole tithe into the storehouse, that there may be food in my house. Test me in this, "says the LORD Almighty, "and see if I will not throw open the floodgates of heaven and pour out so much blessing that there will not be room enough to store it."*

Here are some stories about how God has blessed me by protection and financially through tithing.

Avoided Potential Danger through Tithing

One day, I was at a shopping mall on the 1st day of a month. During that time as I was a new Christian, I did not have anyone to go to church with as almost all of the people around me were Buddhist. So I only gave tithings through donation box at shopping malls.

While I was having lunch at KFC in the mall, I remembered that I had to give tithing. So I took about 3 – 5 minutes to walk to and back from the donation stands and gave tithings. Nothing extraordinary happened. After lunch, I went to the parking lot, drove out of the mall and very unbelievably, saw a burning car with flames all over it on the road that I was supposed to take. I found out that it only happened a while ago. I would surely have somehow gotten involved in it or at least gotten stuck for a very long time on the road if I hadn't spent abt 4 minutes giving tithing.

God has been so good with me financially too, and something always turns up whenever I need anything desperately in my life.

Given In Times of Need

It was the end of high school for all my classmates and me, so we organized a high school formal party for ourselves at a big grand hotel and the ticket for it cost $90. It was the end of the month, and I had no money left to spend on anything when I found out that the party ticket cost $90. I would have already bought it immediately if I had the money as I have seen so many movies of high school senior parties and it looked so fun and cool. I could ask money from my mother, but I did not want to as I didn't want to be looked at as a son who wastes money. So I just stayed quiet and prayed about it. It was already a week before the tickets are no longer sold and I just trusted God to provide for me in some way, somehow. Then just a few days before the tickets are sold no more, my mum surprisingly said that my aunt gave me pocket-money as a reward for my good IGCSE exam score, and I got $100! I was so amazed. The next day, I immediately bought the ticket and was left with $10 (10% of the pocket-money) to tithe too. The high school senior party was the best party that I have ever attended.

Immediate Financial Blessing after Tithing

My parents back in Myanmar lives in a residential apartment where they own some of the apartments there which they rent to people. One day, my mum called me and told me that one particular apartment has not been rented for such a long time and asked me to pray for it. As she was not a Christian at that time, I told her I would ask God for the apartment to be rented within a week's time. However, I only prayed for God's will to be done for the apartment instead of my Family's will. I knew the apartment was not going to be rented within a week, but I asked God to at least give us a sign that he was working towards it. So seven days later, my mum called me and said: "hey, the apartment has not been rented yet." I told her not to worry and that God's plan for us is always better than our plans. Then later she said "but people are staying there for the night, your uncle's family" I assumed it was just God giving us signs that he was working on it.

My parents visited us in April, and we even visited Hillsong Church together on Sunday morning. There was a "prayer box" in the foyer to which my mother wrote for the apartment to be rented and I was sure it was going to be rented very soon. On the 1st Sunday of May 2018, I got much pocket-money, and so I put $100 for tithing on Sunday, trusting that God will continue to provide for my family and me even more. The next day on Monday, my mum called me and said: "The apartment has been rented!" I was so amazed at how God kept showing us exciting miracles every day!

Tithing is not a waste of money people. Honor God, and he will reward you back. God is also a very faithful God and always keeps his promises to us and will never fail us. Even though sometimes, it may look like he isn't doing anything at the moment when it is taking so long for something to happen. Just have faith because God is working for us in the background that we cannot see yet but will only understand later when the miracle comes.

> *Numbers 23:19 "God is not human, that he should lie, not a human being, that he should change his mind. Does he speak and then not act? Does he promise and not fulfill?"*

> *Joshua 21:45 "Not one of all the LORD's good promises to Israel failed; every one was fulfilled."*

He gives you so many amazing promises for your life if you only choose to accept Jesus and have a good relationship with God.

> *Mark 11:24 "Therefore I tell you, whatever you ask for in prayer, believe that you have received it, and it will be yours."*

Chapter 4

God's Unfailing Love

Come Back To God

Well, all of us aren't perfect, and as a new Christian, I didn't have such strong faith yet and easily ran away from God whenever I did something bad again, feeling very guilty about it, being ashamed to come back to God.

Along my journey with God, I at one point got very distant from God and continued to live in sin every-day. Very faithfully one night, God gave me another dream. In the dream, I had committed a terrible crime and was in court.

The judge asked me if I had committed that terrible crime. I said "no!" as I was so afraid to go to jail, wasting my whole life away. However, there was a security camera footage of me committing the crime which they were about to check very soon. I was definitely going to jail.

There was no escape for me at all. I was so scared to death, and I was going to jail anyway, so I got nothing to lose and confessed my crimes. "I did it…" in the court, and I escaped! (by waking up in real life). It was like God was telling me to just confess my sins and come back to him. And the dream only faded away immediately after I said "it" in "I did it." God is such a loving and caring God, even still asking me to come back to him instead of being angry after I ran away from him.

Jesus describe God's unfailing and never-ending powerful love in Luke 15: 11-31

It's a story about a wealthy man's two sons. The younger son who didn't love his father was only after his rich inheritance that he even asked for his share of the estate. Out of love, the father gave his son the part of the property. So as expected, the younger son went away and spent all the money he had on evil things. Only afterward, he realized he had nothing left and had his own needs to fulfill such as hunger. Then he remembered that even his Father's hired servants had food to eat and thought of going back to his Father, apologize and ask for a position of being one of the hired servants to fulfill his hunger. His expectation of his father's kindness was very low.

This is how he prepared to apologize to his father

> *Luke 15: 18-19 "I will set out and go back to my father and say to him: Father, I have sinned against heaven and you. I am no longer worthy to be called your son; make me like one of your hired servants.'"*

So, with a fully prepared apology speech, he went back to his father, thinking that his father would 'at most' give him the position of a hired servant. Then, this happened.

> *Luke 15: 20"But while he was still a long way off, his father saw him and was filled with compassion for him; he ran to his son, threw his arms around him and kissed him."*

The father saw him while he was still a long way off! Meaning that the father was continually looking out for him even though he knew that his son didn't love him and once he saw his son, he ran! Hugged and kissed him!. That is the same expression of love as how God loves you. Even though you may be a long way off, he is always looking out for you, and once you take just one step towards him, he runs to you with only the intention of loving you and making you prosper in all areas of life.

Notice that the son hadn't even spoken a word of his apology speech when the father did that. In our human standard of love, the father would only have a straight face, scold him first, forgive him after he had given a very long apology and only show his love after a week. Unfortunately, due to our experiences in life with people, this happens to be what we think of what God is like, being judgmental with a straight face when we sin. However, it is not like that at all.

The story later goes on saying that after the father embraced him, the son spoke his apology speech but even though he hadn't finished his speech, the father put on the best robe on him, a ring on his finger, sandals on his feet and had a feast for celebrating his son's return. The father was not interested in the son's apology at all because he had already forgiven his son in his heart and was only looking to bless his son with everything else he had as he loved him so much.

Keep in mind that God's love is entirely different from a human's standard of love. Humans' standard of love has a limit. If we do something to a person and they are pushed over their limit of patience, they will never love us again. However, God's love has no limits! No matter what we do, even if we had used Jesus' name as a curse word, he is still looking out for us only to embrace us with his love for us to know the true nature of him and have a deep relationship with him. When Adam sinned, it was not obligatory for God to send his son down to die at the cross for us. God could have just left us to die and be separated from his love forever, but he chose out of love to sacrifice his son at the cross for us while we were still sinners so that he can embrace his love for us through Jesus Christ and let us have a relationship with him.

> **Romans 8:38-39** *"For I am convinced that neither death nor life, neither angels nor demons, neither the present nor the future, nor any powers, neither height nor depth, nor anything else in all creation, will be able to separate us from the Love of God that is in Christ Jesus our Lord."*

Why God First Before Love?

After some time being in college, I was single and started to see many couples being in love so very romantically with each other and felt lonely. I also wanted love but was looking for it in all the wrong places. One day, I got rejected by some and accepted by many. Yet at the end of the day, it felt like there was no real genuine love for me. I was also again a bit distant from God during that time as I was going through emotional roller coasters all the time.

One day, I got back home and was very upset about not being able to find love in life and took a nap being very depressed. In my nap, I had a very interesting dream.

In the dream, I was walking in a very crowded place. Somehow I felt so exhausted and there was so much sweat around my body that when I looked in the mirror of a building beside me, I saw my face was red and full of sweat. Then, I felt so extremely dizzy that I couldn't see my face in the mirror any longer and I fell backward flat on my back. I then saw an elderly lady walking to me and stood close to me, looking down at me being concerned. I felt like as if I was dying and my consciousness was slowly fading away. In a much-weakened voice, I said to the lady "Help... me... " And then I felt so thirsty, so I also said "Water... please... "

After saying that, my consciousness left my body in the dream and I found myself in a very dark cave.

In there, I could hardly see anything at all, and I heard a man shouting so loudly "Jesus! Jesus!" from the other side of the cave and it echoed that I heard the name "Jesus" so loudly some more times.

When I woke up, I opened my phone to go to the internet to search for the meaning of the dream that I had. This is the most fascinating experience that I ever had so far. When I opened my phone and clicked the internet app, a picture that contained a Bible verse immediately popped up.

The verse that popped up was **John 6:35(ESV)**

> *"Jesus said to them, 'I am the bread of life; whoever comes to me shall not hunger, and whoever believes in me shall never thirst."*

How incredible, just when I said "water please" in my dream, the verse said, "shall never thirst." God is good, always watching over us and always trying to put us on the right path again whenever we're going the wrong way.

What caught my eye from this verse was "I am the bread of life."

Imagine when you haven't eaten the whole day, and you finally eat buffet at night. You feel so very satisfied at mind and especially in your stomach physically. Jesus said, "I am the bread of life." Our lives will finally have a real purpose and satisfaction if we decide to follow him and see what he has in store for us. God's plans for us are always so much greater than we can imagine.

> *Matthew 6:33 "But seek first the kingdom of God and his righteousness, and all these things will be given to you as well."*

> *Matthew 10:39, Jesus said: "Whoever finds their life will lose it, and whoever loses their life for my sake will find it."*

Chapter 5

He's Our Best Doctor

Supernatural Healing

A week after I arrived in Melbourne for studying in college, I experienced an excruciating headache for some reasons. It hurt whenever I moved my head quickly, and every single time I get up from bed. I took medicine regularly for it about a week, but it did no good and had no effect at all.

One day, I just gave up on healing myself with medicines and just trusted fully on the LORD. I stopped taking medication that day and just spent my day reading the Bible, listening to sermons and Christian songs. I then prayed for the healing of my headache. I rested fully, taking a nap and trusting God with my headache.

During the nap, I had a dream that I was in a kingdom. Somehow the king died suddenly, and for some reasons, I was to be crowned king of that kingdom. I was so happy and the first one whom I called to tell that I was about to be crowned King was Albert, my best friend. During the Coronation ceremony when I kneeled down, and a crown was being placed on my head, I woke up.

When I woke up, it was a miracle. I did not have any headaches anymore as and my head felt so refreshed and light as if I just got out of the shower. The first one whom I told about the dream I had was Albert, and only after then I realized that he was also the first one in my dream whom I had called to tell that I was about to be crowned king.

Psalm 132:18 (ESV)"His enemies I will clothe with shame. But upon himself his crown will shine".

You Rest, God Heals

It was a typical morning during one of my college days. Everything was going very well until I got on the tram to go to college. While I was standing in the tram, suddenly I felt a very sharp and explosive pain in my back for a few seconds. It was so painful that it caused my knees to bend as a reaction as I couldn't stand straight with the pain. The seconds of sudden pain shocks happened every 10 to 15 minutes. I was thinking about why I was going through that pain and didn't understand why God would let this happen to me. That was my problem; I was focusing on the pain, being worried about it instead of focusing on Jesus.

When I was walking to college along the usual path, I saw a van with a very big word "Grace" painted red on the side from the back end to the front end of the van. That was the first time I've ever seen that van there even though I had been using that path for some months. I wasn't sure if that was just a coincidence or if God was telling me about his grace.

I endured the pain through class and on my way back, I saw a very big "cross" shadow right beside me. I've always used that path but never had seen that big "cross" or the "Grace" Van before. I felt as though God was telling me/ giving me signs that I just needed to trust in him completely and receive his grace freely instead of doubting why the pain happened to me. When I got back home, I rested all my worries and pain in Jesus. I said some prayers over my back as I have healing through Jesus' sacrifice on the cross and I took a nap. When I woke up, the pain was completely gone! Praise the lord! I have been aware that the van car and the big cross shadow might just have been coincidences. So I've been checking every day ever since but never have I ever seen the "cross" shadow or the "Grace" van ever again.

"I am the LORD who heals you" (Exodus 15:26).

Jeremiah 30:17 "'I will restore you to health and heal your wounds,' declares the LORD,"

Isaiah 53:5 "But he was wounded for our transgressions, he was bruised for our iniquities: the chastisement of our peace was upon him; by his stripes, we are healed"(KJV)

1 Peter 2:24 "Who his own self bare our sins in his own body on the tree, that we, being dead to sins, should live unto righteousness: by whose stripes ye were healed."(KJV)

If anybody that's reading this needs healing, God wants to help! Jesus already took your sins and diseases on himself on the cross so that you could be healed.

Chapter 6

Unbelievable Experiences!

An Amazing Dream Came True

During late December of 2017, I had a dream that somehow my mother got a very big pet elephant. The elephant was so big, and it was pregnant too! Later in the dream, it gave birth to 5 baby elephants, and they were all running around very happy with each other.

I remembered the dream in exact details when I woke up. So I searched on the Internet about what elephants in dreams represented. The Internet said it represented prosperity. I was wondering what would happen and didn't really believe in it. However, I called my mother and told her about the dream that I had of her and the elephants.

She was amazed to hear about the dream and also told her brother about it too. Then my mum and uncle bought lottery tickets to test it and told me about it. I just thought they had wasted money on it and didn't believe my dream at all and that it was only my mind playing tricks.

On 1st Jan of 2018, she called me saying that she had won $100 and was very pleased about it. I was happy for her but thought there had to be something more since there were 6 elephants altogether in the dream that I had. On the second day of 2018, my mum called me again, and to my surprise, she told me that my uncle won $500! It was just as the same numbers of the elephants that I had in my dream the month before.

These are the kind of dreams that God gives when you follow him. It's either guidance, a warning or a gift but everything is for your own good.

To analyze it a bit in details, my mum had the pregnant big elephant at first and out of it came 5 baby elephants (which were going to be the same size as the mother elephant when they grow up, so I guessed the value of each of the babies were the same as the mother elephant). So my mum told the good news to my uncle which I think was giving the chance to have five baby elephants ($500) and he took it with good faith. Haha.

I just also had a very good thought about how it felt when I accepted Jesus and the Holy Spirit touched me.

Imagine yourself in a sweltering hot room, and you're sweating. But then you found a refrigerator. So you stand in front of it, and when you open the door, the coldness feels so good and refreshing when it passes over and around your body. It's just like opening a refrigerator inside your body when your body is full of worries and stress because of your everyday activities at work or home. The refreshing feeling will take over your whole body even to the bones and make you feel spiritually alive more than you have ever felt.

It doesn't just end with feeling good. It's mainly about finally having an everlasting relationship with God and receiving his grace your whole life every day. What people fear most nowadays is dying, and you also won't feel afraid of death anymore as Jesus had already conquered death and had shown us what a body in heaven is like. Only then you will know your body on Earth is just a vehicle to drive you around but when you die, you only leave your body and will be living in heaven so peacefully and happily forever with your loving father, God.

Everyone has their own sins just as we have dirt everywhere on our own body and Jesus is the shower for all our dirty sins we committed. Anyone who says "I have never sinned and don't need Jesus" is just as one who says "I am 100% completely clean and I don't need a shower". All of us have our own sins, and we need Jesus to cleanse us of all of our sins. You can never clean yourself to be 100% clean because it is not in your nature and we all know it. The sad truth in real life is that most people don't acknowledge that they are dirty and that they need a shower. Those are the people who claim that they know everything and would only depend on themselves for the afterlife.

> ### *John 9:39 "Jesus said 'For judgment, I have come into this world so that the blind will see and those who see will become blind.'"*

Those who humbly acknowledge they have their own sins and depend on Jesus for their lives, they will finally know the truth of life and see everything that is reality instead of being blinded of the truth by wealth, power or fame like so many people in the world today.

Prayer Unbelievably Answered Immediately

I woke up with a very painful toothache one day, and it hurt very much whenever I touched the affected tooth with my tongue. The worst thing was that it was one of the teeth from the middle of the front row. I couldn't even touch the tooth with my tongue. I thought it was only because I had in some way slept the night pressing against the tooth. Thinking that somehow it was just temporary and would fade away soon, I went to college that day.

It was already 1 p.m., and the pain did not go away as I thought it would. I endured the pain through class and during the lunch break, I went into the toilet and prayed. I prayed, asking for the healing of my toothache just as God has healed me before for my back pain and headache. However, only the day before, I was reading Hillsong's Senior Pastor Brian Houston's latest book; "There is more." There, he mentioned that the common mistake that most people make is that they pray for things that they can easily do. For example, if a toy bear is right in front of you on the table, you don't pray for the toy to somehow jump into your hands but you have to reach out your hand and take it by yourself using your own efforts.

So then I thought it was the same situation with me and my toothache problem because I could simply go to the dental clinic after college for it but the problem was that I was still so scared to go to the dental clinic as it had always been one of my childhood fears, besides cockroaches.

I was also not sure if God would heal me supernaturally or if he wanted me to go to the dentist. The best thing about God is that you can talk to him as your very good friend instead of using such words that differentiate your and his level such as like saying "By your high majestic grace, I hereby present myself to you."

I talked very openly to God like he's my best friend. I told him I did not know what to do. Whether to wait for his supernatural healing or if he wanted me to go to the dental clinic, telling him I'm also very terrified of going to the dental clinic. I told him I was very stuck not knowing what to do between 2 things.

So I asked him to give me any signs or just tell me what to do. "Wait for your supernatural healing or do you want me to go to the dental clinic?" So I took some minutes alone in the toilet praying for guidance.

Then I got out of the toilet and went to a lecture immediately as I was already a few minutes late. I usually sat beside my good friends, but as I was late that day, there weren't any good seats left for me near my friends. So I sat beside a girl that I hadn't met before, at the back of the class. As I'm always very friendly at college and talk to everyone near me, I spoke to her. We introduced each other, and when I asked what her dream job is, she answered "Dentist! Since I was a little kid!" My mind was blown away. I looked up at the ceiling of the room, sighed saying "OK God, you're so amazing. Thank you, Jesus!"

God answered my prayer right immediately after I prayed asking for guidance and just gave me a clear sign for me to go to the dental clinic myself. I have always been so afraid of going to the dental clinic my whole life, but I plucked up my courage and did what God told me to do. And whenever you obey God, only good things come out of it. So the dentist performed a root canal treatment on my tooth, but it did not hurt even a bit as he injected morphine into the gum before the procedure. I was singing Christian songs over and over again in my mind while the dentist was performing the treatment. Everything went fine, and there was no more pain in my tooth anymore the next morning. Thank God for dentists!

The only thing that was fascinating and unbelievable was the perfect timing of everything!

The only day that I had a painful toothache was the only day I met a student who wants to be a dentist for the first time of my life and I only met her right immediately after praying for guidance.

Proverbs 3: 5-6 "Trust in the LORD with all your heart and lean not on your own understanding; in all your ways submit to him, and he will make your paths straight."

Psalms 48: 14 "For this God is our God for ever and ever; he will be our guide even to the end."

Psalms 32: 8 *"I will instruct you and teach you in the way you should go; I will counsel you with my loving eye on you."*

Psalms 34: 17 *"The righteous cry out, and the Lord hears them; he delivers them from all their troubles.*

Maung Maung Kyaw Zaw Hein

Chapter 7

Perfect Timings In Life!

This is one of the most awesome experiences I've had so far when going through life peacefully along with the Holy Spirit and how God even uses little things that we do to lead us to a big purpose

On the 22nd of February, there was a sports club fair at my college from around 9 a.m. to 3 p.m. I always usually had my lunch around 12 but only had it at about 2 p.m. that day as I was looking through the sports clubs at the fair.

While I was having lunch, a guy called Harvey approached me and asked me to fill a survey that he was collecting. The study was mainly about religions, how well we know about it and who Jesus Christ is to us. After finding out he was also a Christian, we had a long talk about how good God is and how he has impacted and changed our lives for good. We wanted to talk more about it, but I had class, so we appointed to meet at a coffee shop on Sunday afternoon.

I couldn't sleep well on Saturday night but still went to Hillsong Church on Sunday morning. I was already a bit sleepy and wanted to cancel my appointment with Harvey. However, I thought about what God would have wanted me to do and what I wanted to do. I wanted to serve God all the time and thought about doing something concerning with Christianity on a Sunday afternoon would be better than sleeping at home and wasting precious time. When I arrived at the coffee shop very early before Harvey, I found out that there was a very big Japanese festival going on around there at the Federation Square. I was just curious, so I walked around and found a Gundam Toy Shop! It's like a Japanese robot toy.

I had been looking for it for a very long time and wanted to buy a Gundam toy for my best friend, Albert as he loves those Gundam toys. I've wanted to buy it for him for so many months but didn't have enough pocket money and also could not find any Gundam Toy Stores around wherever I went to Melbourne in the past. Luckily, February was the month of my birthday, and I had enough pocket money to buy it for Albert. I somehow felt as if God just put me there at the Japanese festival to buy the toy for Albert at the right place and the right time, led by the Holy Spirit.

So I felt the need to buy it and bought it immediately after asking what size Albert's current Gundam Toy was so that I could buy a bigger size Gundam toy for him. I told him God bought it for him through me. He was so surprised and texted me back saying "Really? I've been praying to God for it!" I remember that I texted him back saying "Well, prayers answered ☺"

However, there was only one problem; he was still living back in Myanmar while I was in Australia. I was thinking of sending the Gundam toy to him by post, but it would have cost me a lot as the Gundam toy box was really big. Then my mum texted me saying that my aunt was coming to Melbourne in a few days. So I asked my aunt if she would be fine carrying the Gundam toy box for me all the way back to Myanmar and she very kindly agreed to help out.

During that time, I was (still am) a member of the Trinity College Christian team and we planned to hold a dinner party next Wednesday at the college church for all the college students there and to introduce them to a loving God after dinner. I was responsible for writing a letter inviting them to stay after dinner so that we can tell them about Christianity. I wrote it very nicely and gave it to the college Chaplain, Heather who is an amazing woman of God, planned everything for the party and planned to type the letter in and print it to give it to everyone at the party.

Back to the Gundam toy, I went to my cousin's place where my aunt was staying and gave the Gundam toy to her. On my way back while walking, I came across a Christian stall and as always, I checked to see what they were doing and offering. The people there were so generous and gave me DVDs like "Evolution vs. God," some booklets to help understand Christianity and a "Father's Love Letter" letter.

As I got back home that day, I read the Father's Love Letter, which is like a love letter from God to everyone, which is all made up of Bible verses expressing God's love for each and every one of us. It came straight to my heart that I had to use that one instead of the one that I had written for the party to invite everyone to stay after dinner. So on that Saturday night, I emailed the gentleman from the Christian Stall, asking if I could have 200 of those Father's Love letters for the party and asked when I could have it As Soon As Possible.

The next morning, he emailed me back telling me that he got those letters instead of making them and had to ask someone of the main source about it. On Monday, he emailed me again but so surprisingly said that he already got the 200 Father's Love Letters and that I can have it on Wednesday afternoon! (and the party was at night!). Such perfect timings when flowing along with the Holy Spirit's guidance. So I met up with him during the afternoon on Wednesday and got the 200 letters that I had asked for. When I got to the party, Heather told me she had forgotten to write and print out what I wrote for invitation letter after dinner, but I had my 200 Father's Love Letter s as backup and succeeded in giving out so many love letters to many people who came to the party at the college church. There were even three salvations, it was all worth it, and I would do it all over again and again for more. I also found out that my best friend, Albert had just received the Gundam Toy the day before and he was so happy and pleased about it.

The next week on Wednesday at the same college church, I gave a speech about how I got the Love Letters and that I would not have gotten it if I just had chosen to sleep instead of meeting up with Harvey for coffee on a Sunday afternoon. Many people there were amazed by it, and some came to me, telling me that they kept coming to the church because they were touched by the Father's Love Letters which I gave out the week before. It melted my heart out of happiness as I was extremely pleased to hear that they were so touched by the Words of God, which expressed God's love for them.

All of this definitely would not have been possible if I had not met Harvey or just made the choice to go back home and sleep on that Sunday afternoon instead of meeting up with Harvey. The chances of all this happening in perfect timing was just actually a true miracle for me.

This is a summary of what happened

- Met Harvey during lunch

- Found out there was a Gundam toy store near the appointed coffee shop

- Perfect time to buy Gundam Toy for Albert

- Albert's prayer answered

- Found out aunt was coming to Melbourne in a week

- Received gifts and the Father's Love Letter when going back home from aunt's home

- Receiving the 200 Letters right on the day of the party just in time for the party at night

- Albert's Gundam toy delivered to his house the day before the party.

- Heather forgot to write/print the letters I had written, but I had the backup Father's Love Letters

- Everyone at the party received Love Letters from God

That's what happens when you walk with the Holy Spirit alongside guiding you in every step of your life. Being sensitive to the Holy Spirit is important. How can you be sensitive to the Holy Spirit and walk closely alongside him every day? Here's the answer (I think).

Romans 12: 2 "Do not conform to the pattern of this world, but be transformed by the renewing of your mind. Then you will be able to test and approve what God's will is—his good, pleasing and perfect will."

Don't let your mind be occupied with any worries or stress. Renew it.

Chapter 8

God's Guidance through Dreams

Giant Snake in a Museum

It was on the day that I had a college math exam. The night before, I had a very interesting dream.

In my dream, my family and I were at a huge museum where there was full of people. Suddenly, an enormous sized snake came slithering around in the museum near us as if it already knew the place so well like it was at home. This giant snake's body diameter was up to my chest, and its length would be around 100 feet long. People in the museum were frightened and were running away from the snake. But somehow I was not afraid of the snake at all and was even petting the snake. It also did me no harm and got along with me so well. It was so big that my family had to climb to the top floor of the museum to take a picture of me putting my hands on the giant snake. When I left the museum, the first person I showed the picture to was my best friend, Albert.

When I woke up, I did not remember the dream in full details, and as usual, I told Albert about the dream that I had of the giant snake and then only remembered that he was the first one I showed the picture in the dream. In reality, he was also the first one I told about the dream and the description of the giant snake's size.

As usual, I went to the Internet to search about the dream meaning of snakes, and it says that the giant snake represented a big problem but it was friendly with me and I was not scared. So the interpretation was that I would have a big problem in real life, but I wouldn't be scared of it at all. The big problem, in real life, would do me no harm even though it looked so dangerous.

On that day, I had my college math exam at 12: 30 p.m. It was raining very heavily, and so I left my home at 11: 30 a.m. To my shock, as there was also a Grand Prix car race event that time, the trams did not go as far as my destination to the university campus. It stopped in the middle of the road and drove backward. But I was listening to Christian songs very loudly with earphones and was taking a nap, so I did not hear or know anything about the tram going backward. I also never knew that the tram goes backward on special occasions. I had no idea what was going on when I woke up, and my first thought was "Hold on, I'm sure that I took the tram that goes to the university campus. Why is it going backward? Have I somehow been teleported into the other tram route that goes backward? I don't also remember myself getting off and taking another tram too. What's going on?"

It was already 12 in the afternoon when I finally understood what happened and what was going on. That was also when I realized that I had forgotten to bring my exam ticket! In addition, I did not know where the exam hall was on campus so it also would have taken me some time to find the exam hall. I was in shock and did not know what to do. I got off the tram to walk and got on another on which gets me to the campus. But I also needed to go somewhere and print the exam ticket, and it would have cost me 10 or 15 minutes. I was in a very stressful situation, not knowing what to do. I was worried, thinking if I should print my exam ticket or try my luck to see if I can get inside the exam hall without exam ticket but time was also running out for me.

Then I remembered the giant snake dream that I had the night before, and I remembered to stay very calm even though there's a very big problem for me going on at that moment. So when I got out of the 1st tram, I thought I had screwed up already. So I did the only thing I could think of. I prayed to God asking for guidance and help for about a minute. I prayed like "Lord, I don't understand why you allowed this to happen to me. Do you want me to go back home and miss my exam for some reasons or do you want me to keep going? Please give me just a sign or anything to lead me where to go."

Some seconds after I had prayed, I kept walking to the 2nd tram being sensitive to any signs that would indicate me to keep going or turn back. Then I immediately met one of the college students who also happened to forget his ticket, telling me that we don't need it (gave me peace and relaxation inside). He even knew where the exam hall was, so I just followed him along to the exam hall and unbelievably, everything went 100% fine! Which I thought was impossible.

Again, the fascinating thing was that I would not have met him if I hadn't taken some time to pray to God for help. I believe God gave me the dream to tell me that if I stay calm even though the problem around me looks so scary and dangerous, it won't do me any harm.

So when you have such big problems everywhere around you in life, the only and best thing you can do is to pray to God for help or guidance and he will always answer. Those who joyfully leave everything in God's hand will eventually see God's hand in everything. The giant in front of you is never bigger than the God inside of you.

Nowadays, many people lose their faith in God when they are in big trouble, and they only depend on their own strength and forget to rely on God. That's when the test of faith really is. Will you rest, leaving all your problems to God or will you stress yourself out trying to solve it by yourself, forgetting God?

When we're in big trouble, it's the most crucial time to have more faith in God. Why? It's like this.

Imagine you're taking a train journey to somewhere far. On the way, you see beautiful scenery and landscapes when you go on top of mountains and hills. You feel so positively happy, energetic and refreshed. Then later, you go through into a dark tunnel. Suddenly, there's an earthquake. Many stones start falling from above, and the train shakes frequently. It's like the tunnel is about to collapse. You feel very nervous and scared, but the worst thing you can do is to jump 'out' of the train in hopes of trying to make a run for the exit a long way by your own strength. That is even the exact time that you stay seated with seat belts on in the train, seated securely to make it out of the tunnel alive. The good news is, the train you're on is indestructible and will keep you alive even if the tunnel collapsed. This train will somehow magically pull out giant drills in the front and drill its way out of the collapsed tunnel for your well-being. Miracles happen if you still have strong faith even when there are problems all around you. All you need to do is to remain in peace and trust God with everything going on around you.

That's the same concept with God. Even though there are problems everywhere in your life, focus on Jesus, and everything will be fine in the end no matter how impossible it may look like. The good news is that you can trust and rely on God 100% with all your heart and he will never fail or disappoint you.

> *Romans 10:11 "As Scripture says, "Anyone who believes in him will never be put to shame."*

> *Psalms 37:4-5 "Take delight in the Lord, and he will give you the desires of your heart. Commit your way to the Lord; trust in him and he will do this."*

> *Matthew 14:26-31 "When the disciples saw him walking on the lake, they were terrified. "It's a ghost!" they said and cried out in fear. But Jesus immediately said to them "take courage! It is I. Don't be afraid". "LORD, if it is you." Peter replied, "tell me to come to you on the water." "Come," he said. Peter got down out of the boat, walked on the water and came towards Jesus. But when he saw the wind, he was afraid and beginning to sink, cried out, "Lord, save me!" Immediately Jesus reached out his hand and caught him. "You of little faith," he said, "why did you doubt?"*

Many of us are like Peter in this situation. When there's no problem in life, we have such strong faith, but then we lose our faith immediately when a problem occurs around us and shakes our faith. That's when we start to focus on the problem instead of focusing on Jesus. Peter began to sink only when he focused on and became worried about the wind, but he was doing perfectly fine walking on water when he had all his attention on Jesus. Jesus said "Don't be afraid" many times to people around him. Don't be afraid, stand firm in faith and you will always overcome every obstacles and trouble in your life when you walk closely with God every day in your life.

> *Mark 5:36 (NLT) "But Jesus overheard them and said to Jairus "Don't' be afraid. Just have faith".*

Therefore, don't be afraid of all the problems in your life and don't hold tight onto all those problems trying to solve it with only your own strength. Have no worries, let the problems be transferred to the LORD and he will take care of it for you. All you need to do is have faith.

The phrase "don't be afraid" is written in the Bible 365 times! Coincidence? I think not! That's God telling us not to be afraid every day of our lives and trust in him with everything in life

> *Matthew 6:33 "But seek first his kingdom and his righteousness, and all these things will be given to you as well."*

God will give you everything you want in life simply if you trust in him, follow him and put him first before everything! It would be hard for unbelievers to believe but please, take a leap of faith in him and see the results for yourself.

Driving A Car With Bad Brakes

There was a time I conflicted with myself over two choices in life. I had the chance to choose both, but I thought it would not be right of me to do that as I was only thinking of accepting one and rejecting the other choice.

Then I had a dream one night where in my dream, I was driving a big car with bad brakes. I had to get to a place so quickly in my dream as it was an emergency situation. However, when I got into the car and was driving to get to the emergency place, I had very little control over the car as it took about 5 seconds for the car to stop completely after I hit the brake. But then I found myself in a room as if seeing me driving the car was just to show me what would have happened if I were to drive the car. Then I found a man in the same room as me who had the car keys. Even though I had seen what would have happened if I drove, I still asked for the car keys from the man (whom I could not see the face), but he always refused and never gave me the car keys in my dream.

When I woke up, I immediately knew God was telling me not to depend on myself for the situation and just let him take control. Even though I was scared, I just gave that problem to God and did nothing about it. Everything just went fine for me in the end as if the problem was actually as small as a seed.

It was like the dream was just guidance for me in real life. It was telling me what would happen if I had acted on my thoughts, I would've hurt someone. But let God take the problem for you, and he will always solve it for you. You don't need to worry about anything at all.

I think when the man in my dream refused to give me the car keys, I think it was God telling me like "Do not drive the car, let me drive it for you. Just trust me." What an amazing God we have.

"Be still and know that I am God" (Psalm 46:10).

Bitten By a Snake

In this dream that God gave me, I was living in a basement of a house, and somehow, many snakes entered into my bedroom while I was occupied, and when I looked around, there were snakes everywhere. I moved around very slowly between all of the snakes in the room, but one particular snake came directly straight at me. It struck at me a few times, chased me into the corner and kept striking at me when I fell down. However, while it was striking at me, I was praying in tongues and could avoid all of its countless strikes at me. Then I quickly caught the aggressive snake by its head with my hands. When releasing it into a box to contain it, it accidentally bit my palm while it was falling into the box. I did not know if the snake was venomous or not, but when I started to worry too much, the blood vessels in my right arm became thick black! The venom was taking its effect, and I was so scared in the dream. But then when I calmed down and kept peace inside, the blood vessel turned back to a healthy green color as if there wasn't even any venom in the system anymore.

Within 24 hours after waking up, out of all the problems (snakes) that I had in my life, one particular problem struck at me. I was so worried about it and was so stressed out. However, I calmed down and kept peace inside. Then I was not worried at all, and the problem went away so quickly as if it never happened.

God was showing me that a problem will happen to me, but it will not have its effect on me negatively if I have peace inside.

Chapter 9

A Familiar Voice

In May 2018, I was already so passionate about knowing all about Jesus and serving him with all my heart and soul because I had finally found a true purpose in my life. I listened to Christian songs and sermons all the time, but the basic thing that I didn't do regularly was to read the words of God, which is the Bible. People suggested me to read starting from the New Testament but I wanted to know everything from start to end, and so I started reading all the way from the book of Genesis (the first book in the Bible which consists of 66 books). I was so hungry to know more and more about God every-day. Then during the few days when I was reading the book of 'Kings', I had a dream one night.

In the dream, I was outside at night with the moon shining brightly. I saw a very tall building as if it almost reached the sky. And suddenly, the building was on fire, and then a strong wind blew from to the left side of me, and I heard a very familiar voice, just as the ones I heard in my past dreams. I was already familiar with it that I was not even scared of it but was also happy to hear it as it was so gentle and soft but clear. Unexpectedly, it said: *"If you want to know me, look at Matthew 1 and read."*

I was very shocked and was thinking like "God, don't I know you already?" But no, now I realized that I just had a relationship with him personally but did not know about him because I have never read the Bible with my heart about Jesus. I just called on Jesus in the time of my trouble "Lord, help me" or "save me from this."

It's like if you have a father who lives away from you but sends you money every month for your needs and you accept the payment. You call him and ask for more when you want or need more. You get the benefits, but you don't know your father personally until you let him talk to you about himself. Usually, when we pray, we are only talking to him about our wants and needs but not listening to what he says for us. We have to spend time in the word of God, the Bible, for God to be able to speak to us through his words in the Bible. People always ask "If God exists, let him speak to me directly" and he already did through the Bible which are his spoken words that are still very much alive even now. We have to spend time reading the Bible for God to talk to us through his words.

Immediately I found out that the Book of Matthew is the first book of the New Testament, chapter 1 being about the birth of Jesus. So I dived right in, reading a few chapters every-day. It was very exciting because the voice in the dream told me to read Matthew 1 if I want to know about him and Matthew 1 is the chapter of the birth of Jesus.

I was scared that time as I thought I was not even saved as the voice implied that I did not 'know' him. I kept asking God about it, and then only later he revealed to me what he really meant when I read the book "How to hear God's voice" by Mark and Patti Virkler. In the book, they mentioned that

Jesus said, "This is eternal life, that they might know Thee, the only true God and Jesus Christ whom Thou hast sent" (John 17:3). The word used here for 'know' is ginosko, and it means, "to be involved in an intimate, growing relationship." It's not the ordinary meaning of the English 'know' that we know! Ha-ha.

I was so surprised and thanked God for revealing it to me. It was only like as if I was saved, I knew him but did not have an intimate, growing relationship with him. God is so good that he guided me to the way to understanding more about him and being in an intimate, growing relationship with him.

Just a few days later, I started to already sink in spiritually with the word of God and the story of Jesus. The Bible was already starting to impact my life and even help me more with everything that I need in my life, even for tiny little things. Here is an example of how God spoke to me through his words in the Bible. It's also by the perfect timing of the Holy Spirit. Simply ask for his guidance in everything, and he will guide you in every step of your life, even the tiny little ones.

College was getting very tough and tiring weeks after weeks. I still was a part of the organization team for my college church party every Wednesday night. One Wednesday morning, I was already tired since I woke up thinking "Man, it's going to be a very long day. I don't even want to go to the church party tonight. But I will do it for Jesus. I wish there were more people there to help me pack up everything". We had been organizing that college church party every night for the past four months. I wanted to tell the chaplain to recruit more people so that I won't have to do much work but I was also worried that she would think I'm lazy. Before I faced the very long day, I decided to pray and read the Bible. While reading Matthew chapter 9 that morning, a particular verse spoke out to me very strongly. That verse was

Matthew 9:37-38 "Then he said to his disciples, "The harvest is plentiful, but the workers are few. Ask the Lord of the harvest, therefore, to send out workers into his harvest field."

Oh yes immediately, I started to meditate on those two verses and asked God for more workers in the college church party, even though I decided not to ask the Chaplain because I was afraid she might think I'm lazy. On that very night at the college church party, nobody except the organization team came! I was astonished because throughout the whole four months, at least 3 or 4 people came even during the worst times. So we discussed how to reach out to more people from college and Heather, the chaplain suggested we recruit more people! I was surprised she even said that as I never expected it. So I told everyone there that those Bible verses Matthew 9:37-38 really spoke out that morning and read them aloud. Then Heather said, "That's what I had just said a while ago!" I didn't hear that as I was distracted. We then got our new dedicated workers after a few weeks and have been working together with them ever since!

Chapter 10

God's Guidance Through The Bible

The Bible had been speaking out to me and giving me almost everything I need for my daily guidance. Here are some examples.

Don't Even Argue

My sister hates Christianity and kept mentioning me in the comments section of a Face-Book page that posts pictures that mock God. She never listened to my explanations and was always thinking of ways to find faults within and to criticize it severely. I really did not like it at all, but of course, I kept praying for her every-day, and I did not also know what to do about her. So I asked God if I should defend my points by arguing with her or ignore her and I read the Bible. Then, surprisingly a verse spoke out to me. It was

Proverbs 9:7 "Whoever corrects a mocker invites insults; whoever rebukes the wicked incurs abuse."

Refrain From Dirty Talks

As I was a college student and had many friends, I also had many friends who were very dirty minded. As I am a very sociable person and am always laughing or smiling everywhere, I talked with almost everyone I see and laugh together with them. Back in school, I was notorious among teachers for smiling even though the teachers were scolding at me. Like come on teachers, scolding is enough, why make a child feel more miserable by taking away his smile from his face? So as I was saying, those college friends were also great friends of mine, but most of the things they were talking about were perverted.

Of course, as I wanted to blend into all the social groups, I usually talked about it and laughed along with them. After I kept reading the Bible daily, I still talked about it with them, always feeling guilty afterwards. I was also not sure if it was ok to laugh with friends about that topic or not. I was thinking like "Am I doing what is wrong in the eyes of the LORD? But it's just a conversation for fun. I mean, everyone jokes about dirty stuff like that every day. I think it's ok and don't think it's a problem. But God, if possible, please show me or tell me what I should do."

So that evening when I got back home, I slept while listening to Pastor Joseph Prince's sermons and there he mentioned

> **Proverbs 4:20-23 "My son, pay attention to what I say; turn your ear to my words. Do not let them out of your sight, keep them within your heart; for they are life to those who find them and health to one's whole body. Above all else, guard your heart, for everything you do flow from it."**

Then he preached by focusing that the words are "life to those who find them and health to one's whole body." It amazed me that God's words are even health to the whole body that I opened my eyes immediately, opened my Bible and highlighted those verses. Then what immediately comes after was

> **Proverbs 4: 24: "Keep your mouth free of perversity; keep corrupt talk far from your lips."**

It amazed me. God just showed me what I asked for right on that day.

Too Much Honey

Having classes at 8 a.m. four days of the week is a terrible thing. What's even worse was having to wake up at 6:30 a.m. to make it on time to classes. I'm also really lazy to wake up earlier to eat breakfast so what I usually did every day before leaving the house was having honey put on two loaves of bread, sticking them against each other and eating them on the way to college. It only took as quick as 30 seconds to prepare, so it was very good for me. So I've always been eating bread with honey regularly, and whenever I go to the grocery store, it's usually always to buy bread and honey ha-ha. One Saturday, I woke up at 1 p.m. after taking a nap and was a bit hungry. I found out that I only had one loaf of bread left and so I put so much honey onto it, folded it in half and ate it. But the honey was spilt so many times every time I took a bite from it. After cleaning the floor, I sat down and read the Bible before doing anything else for the day. Immediately I found this verse

> **Proverbs 25:16 "If you find honey, eat just enough- too much of it, and you will vomit."**

I've been reading only 1 chapter of Proverbs every-day, 1 chapter from the Old Testament from the start and another one from the New Testament starting from Matthew every-day. But how very accurate to what just happened to me. God guides us all the time in everything that we do! We have to let him talk to us through the Bible and be sensitive to the Holy Spirit. Spilt honey because I put too much and finding the Bible verse immediately telling me not to eat too much honey, wow.

Forgiveness

Being a very passionate Christian among a Buddhist family, relatives, and friends is not easy at all. After I posted my baptism video on Facebook, declaring publicly that I became a true Christian, it was a shock to so many of my relatives and friends. Even some of my relatives made fun of me and Jesus. They thought I was just a foolish little kid who got easily persuaded by Christians to become a Christian and I was made fun of and mocked at. In any event, I still kept loving them and praying for them. I felt very sad for them that they did not know how good God is and was making fun of Jesus. One day, I even felt a little bit depressed, but somehow I heard this Bible verse twice in the morning, which I think was the work of the Holy Spirit helping me. The Bible verse was

> **Luke 23: 34 (ESV) "Father, forgive them, for they know not what they do."**

I did not take so much care of hearing that Bible verse even twice that morning as I thought it was just my mind playing tricks on me psychologically. Then in the afternoon, I went to the alpha course class, and the chaplain showed us the weekly alpha course video. In the video, somehow the man mentioned the same Bible verse twice while explaining about forgiveness! It was starting to convince me already. Later at night, there was an evensong service on Thursday night at the college where there was beautiful choir singing which sounded like angels singing. I even had my eyes closed, listening to the songs sung by beautiful voices. Then surprisingly, I heard them singing "Father...forgive them...for they know now what they do!.."

It was a 'WOW' experience because I finally had realized the Holy Spirit was guiding me all the time to hear that one particular Bible verse so that I could finally understand why the people who criticized me did not like me. I was thinking the whole time like Jesus or I did not even do anything bad against them so why would they persecute me like that? The Bible verse that I kept hearing just answered it for me. And yes you guessed it right, it is because they did not know what they were doing. It's very sad, but it's just the way it is. That is also one of the strong reasons that I wrote this book, ha-ha. So that I can finally explain everything to everyone who thinks I was just a little kid who got tricked into converting my religion into Christianity.

This is why if we keep reading the Bible daily, God speaks to us through his words in the Bible whenever we need it. If we don't read it but keep praying daily, it's almost the same as talking to God every day but not allowing him to talk back to us. It becomes a very one-sided conversation which is not so good for the long run in the future.

No matter what you do, there will always be people who are blind to the truth and will keep persecuting you until their spiritual eyes have been opened. These are three very important Bible verses that every Christians should know. Jesus already said in **John 15:18**

"If the world hates you, keep in mind that it hated me first."

2 Corinthians 4:4 (NLT) "Satan, who is the god of this world, has blinded the minds of those who don't believe. They are unable to see the glorious light of the Good News. They don't understand this message about the glory of Christ, who is the exact likeness of God."

Matthew 5:10-12 (ESV) *"Blessed are those who are persecuted for righteousness' sake, for theirs is the kingdom of heaven. "Blessed are you when others revile you and persecute you and utter all kinds of evil against you falsely on my account. Rejoice and be glad, for your reward is great in heaven."*

Before I was a Christian, I have always wondered if there is more to life than just working in the office, getting married, having kids and dying later. It was so black and white for me. I did not even know where I would go when I die in the future. But now, life is so colorful as if I had been blind my whole life. When I was an atheist, I always thought of using a time machine to go into the past to undo all the silly stupid things that I had done that caused me great success in life. There were so many things I regret doing and always wished to turn back in time to correct it. But after becoming a Christian, the relationship with Jesus is so precious and good that I enjoy living every day even though there are bad days too but I never want to go back to the past again because I am enjoying the present time so much with Jesus. During the times of my depression in the past, there was nobody for me, and I had nothing to hope for, and it just made me worse. But now when something bad happens to me, I have peace and rest inside, knowing that God's got my back and not caring about the problem as God will take care of it for me.

Isaiah 49:23 *"You will know that I am the Lord; those who hope in me will not be disappointed."*

Bitterness

I read 1 chapter of the book of "Proverbs" from the Bible every day to gain wisdom as it's written by God through King Solomon who was the wisest man that ever lived, except for Jesus. He was also the richest man that ever lived that if we were to measure his wealth as today's standard, he would be richer than Bill Gates and Mark Zuckerberg combined.

I read a chapter of Proverbs according to the date of the month. For example, if it is 10th today, I read chapter 10 and have been doing it for some months already. Almost every time, a verse speaks out to me for correction or advice for the day.

One night, I had a dream of myself in a dark, dirty storage room with a girl and she kissed me. However, during and after the kiss, my tongue felt so bitter that I couldn't even handle it anymore in the dream and I woke up.

I did not understand the dream immediately even though I asked God for it. Then I asked God again before reading my Bible that morning and read Proverbs chapter 5 as it was 5th of the month that day. The chapter was about warnings against adultery.

And immediately, a Bible verse spoke to me that even relates to my dream.

Proverbs 5:3-4 "For the lips of the adulterous woman drips honey, and her speech is smoother than oil; but in the end, she is bitter as gall, sharp as a double-edged sword."

I was so surprised as in the dream. My tongue tasted such bitterness! And there it was the word that my tongue tasted! So I kept in my mind to refrain from hanging out with any girls that day, and sure enough, one girl from my college who was a friend of mine but was a naughty one with piercings and tattoos asked me to hang out with her! I refused immediately being obedient to God's guidance as I didn't want any trouble.

Revelation in dream

As I kept reading the Bible every day, praying, listening to Christian songs and sermons all the time, I grew much deeper in my relationship with God and got to know him so much better. I understood very well that faith alone is enough for salvation and that works aren't required for salvation as we are saved by grace through faith alone which is the grace of God by sending his son Jesus to die on the cross for us. However, one night as I read the Bible, I read James chapter 2 which explained about faith and works working together and that faith without works is dead using the example of Abraham sacrificing his son from the Old Testament. I knew that it was talking about works being activated by faith, but I was very confused about it, whether it was talking about Abraham's 'work' or his 'faith,' I did not know. So as usual, after reading that chapter and being confused, I just simply asked God to reveal to me the answer that I wanted to know about it and just slept peacefully that night. In the dream, I was in a place somewhere sitting at a table and reading the Bible. A few moments passed by and I had my eyes closed. All I could see was bright light as the room in the dream was brightly lit. Then, I sensed an intense feeling to read "Romans chapter 4" in the dream as if something in the dream just gave me the feeling to read it. So I even woke up that morning saying to myself "must read chapter 4, must read chapter 4". Later I opened my Bible and read Romans chapter 4 and was very surprised to see that Romans chapter 4 was explaining all about 'Abraham being justified by Faith' and not by works. God just gave me the answer to the question I had in the dream! He is always there for us.

> **Romans 4:2-3 "If, in fact Abraham was justified by works, he had something to boast about – but not before God. What does Scripture say? "Abraham believed God, and it was credited to him as righteousness."**

The timing of the dream was so perfect and accurate, and God is always guiding us with his words in the Bible! Our part is to open the Bible and read, letting him speak to us and guide us.

Chapter 11

God's Amazing Plan

God Chose College for Me

God's plans for our lives are so much greater than we can ever imagine for ourselves. Even though the journey would not be as comfortable as we think it would be, we will have everything we truly ever want from the deepest desires of our hearts in the future.

I would like to share with you about my experience in following God's plan for my life, and how good it was compared to the plans I had for myself. This occurred sometime around September 2017.

All my life, I had played chess very competitively since the age of 7 and even achieved the "Fide Master" title in chess at the age of 16 from the Chess Olympiad Tournament 2016 in Baku, Azerbaijan. I was the youngest National Chess Player in my country and was at my top level. I never really studied anything much for my education and only started studying for IGCSE O level exam just a month before I answered it.

The minimum entry requirement to enter into a university in the USA was at least 5 C's. I answered only five subjects and thank God, I got 1A, 2B's and 2C's (not a D!), which was enough for me to enter into an American university, which I had always dreamt of going to.

I wanted to study Zoology that time as I really loved animals so much that I even had a pet corn snake back at home in Myanmar. My dream for my life was to study Zoology, get a job in the US and have so many pets! Especially reptiles! I always love to do what normal people don't usually do. I never wanted to study in Australia because my favorite species of pet snake was the corn snakes and ball pythons which both are illegal to own in Australia! And my sister, who never got along with me since we were kids, was in Australia and I never wanted to be in the same country as her.

Australia was the worst country in my mind for me to go to as those never lined up with the plans I had for myself.

And so it was time for me to start sending applications to enroll into universities. Before everything, I prayed to God first, asking for his guidance in my life and for his will to be done in my life instead of my will because I knew his plans are always greater than the plans I had for myself.

Matthew 10:39 (NLT) "If you cling to your life, you will lose it, but if you give up your life for me, you will find it."

Just after praying about it, my parents arrived home at night, so happily, telling me that they got me into Trinity College, Melbourne, Australia. I was surprised and asked how it was possible. I knew I was not even qualified for it as it required at least 4 out of 6 subjects and I answered only five subjects to make sure I would not be qualified to enter into that college. I knew that if I got qualified, my parents would encourage me to go study and live with my sister, which I feared would have destroyed all the dreams I had for my future life. Before that night, I even remember my aunt asking me "Son, can you still go to Australia to the same college that your sister went to?" and I even answered back "Hah! There is no chance for me to go there because I answered only five subjects and it requires at least 6, don't worry, I made sure of it. I am going to the USA."

So of course, I asked my parents how I got into Trinity, and they said they met the Admission Manager of Trinity College who accepted my sister's admission into the college and told him that I wanted to study at Trinity College too. The Admission Manager said that he would help me and asked my parents and me to meet him at the seminar the next morning. Although I did not want to go to that college, I just went along with my parents to the seminar to see if I would actually really get in as I was not academically qualified for it. Everything went well, and the Admission Manager told me he would help me get into the college that I was actually unqualified to attend at. In my mind, I knew it was God's will for my life as it happened right after my prayer for guidance, but I refused to believe it because it was against 'my' plans for my life.

I actually was testing to see if I would get in or not out of curiosity. And of course, I went to other universities agency centers and enquired about USA universities to study Bachelor of Zoology. But among all the handout book that I read, I noticed that I had no choice but to study chemistry if I were to study at an American university and I really hated chemistry so much. The application process for the American universities also sounded to be very a very complicated process, which was confusing for me, and I hate dealing with complicated issues. The next day, I got an offer letter from Trinity College, Melbourne, Australia which I accepted straightaway out of happiness and excitement that I received an offer letter from a college for the first time of my life. I also did not want to go to the USA anymore as I didn't want to study chemistry and I could choose subjects that I wanted to study in college and so I could omit studying chemistry in college.

After a few weeks, my mind changed again realizing that all the plans I had for my future were all going to be in ruins. I decided I was going to the USA to study Zoology and told my parents I changed my mind. However, they told me they had already prepaid for my Trinity College tuition fees! I was so devastated to know that all my dreams were gone in just a few weeks. I literally begged my parents every day to change their mind and let me go to an American university, but they never changed their mind about it. I even prayed to God like "OK God, please change their mind and allow them to let me go study in the USA. Please! But most importantly, your will be done in my life. If this is where you want me to go, I shall go even though the dreams I imagined for my future is destroyed." Now I realized how unknowingly stubborn I was and not seeing the big picture that God had for me and it always makes me laugh whenever I thought about it. I imagined myself as if I was carrying my own cross and suffering for Christ by sacrificing my dreams. But God had bigger plans for me, plans that he knew I would enjoy so much when going along with it.

Psalm 37:4 "Delight yourself in the LORD, and he will give you the desires of your heart."

That time, I really didn't even know the true desires of my heart, but God knew it, and as I went along with his plans, I never expected my life to be full of happiness and joy, never feeling hollow/lonely/empty in my heart again.

Major That GOD Chose For Me

I arrived in Melbourne, Australia in December 2017 whereas my College program was only going to start in January. I had a month free time to do whatever I liked and to spend more time with God. I explored the college during that month and saw a poster at one of the entrance gates "Study Theology," and I did not even know what Theology was. Only when I knew about it, I told my parents that studying Theology sounds cool! But they didn't allow me to study it as they, even including I thought it was just too crazy of us to study Theology for a Bachelor major as I was not familiar with it at all. I thought only super religious or crazy people study it as it was so strange for me.

One morning during the month, I explored the College brochure, checking out so many majors available to study at the university after my college year. Zoology was there too, but somehow I did not want to study it anymore, and I did not know why too. So I prayed to God that morning, asking what he would want me to study and went about my day. I went to the Melbourne State Library to play chess in the afternoon where I played with an old guy who was really friendly. In the evening, I met him again somewhere else, and we had a short conversation about ourselves and talked about Churches for me to go to. Later he asked, "What are you going to study?" I said that I didn't know yet. Then he immediately said "Study Theology" out of nowhere and told me that it's the best major for me. I was quite surprised, as I had only prayed in the morning, asking God for guidance in my studies.

However, I really still thought it was just too much or too strange/crazy for me and that only really very devoted people study it and make a living with it. I also had a thought in the back of my head that it was really not a secure degree for me to have. But months later, I was already very passionate about Christianity and realized that Zoology was just the least-worst subject I could pick to study as I actually did not really have a passion for it. All I did in my free time during those days was listen to Christian preaching sermons, listen to Christian songs, read the Bible or watch biblical movies and I was somehow already starting to be really interested in studying the Bachelor of Theology.

God-given vision for my future

One night on Sunday, I could not sleep well and was rolling around on the bed. Then I saw a vision that God gave me for the first time. In the vision, I was on the sofa in the living room and had my Ipad open in my hands. The words that were displayed on the Ipad were in 'yellow' color saying "Bachelor of Theology" with the location "Parkville" and more details below all written in yellow color.

But I did not think much of it as I thought it was only an illusion that I had as I never had a vision before. The next day, as I was already so interested in studying Bachelor of Theology, I asked the chaplain to recommend me Theological schools to study for that degree. She recommended me only "Ridley College" and said that it's an excellent Bible college. I forgot about the vision that I had, and so when I got back home, I immediately sat down on my sofa and opened my Ipad to search about Ridley College. There I found the exact same things as I saw in my vision the night before. "Bachelor of Theology" "Location: Parkville" and more details below, all written in yellow color! Then only immediately I knew that God had really been guiding me throughout all the way since he got me accepted into Trinity College. So of course, I told my parents about the vision that I had and asked if I can study "Bachelor of Theology" to which they allowed me to which made me so happy! God is so good. Note that I am still in Trinity College as I am writing this though, ha-ha but my future has been laid out for me very clearly, and I have to go step by step with full of faith in God. I'm also going to surely get an internship working for the college church party starting from next year. I plan to become a pastor and travel around the world, preaching the gospel to so many lost people out there and change their lives completely. But of course, I will go where God wants me to go.

I never imagined that my life in Australia would be this good and I am so blessed to have Heather, the college chaplain who guides me in my walk with God, be part of the Trinity College Church weekly party organization and getting to go to Hillsong Church every Sunday is my favorite! Best of all, by the grace of the holy spirit, I have learned to be patient with my sister, never getting angry at her, always loving her and being able to forgive her immediately when she does something wrong to me (Praise Jesus I am able to do that). She cooks for me, and her boyfriend is an amazing guy who gets along with me so well. I never feel bored at the apartment in Australia anymore and am very happy here. This was the complete opposite of what I had imagined it to be, all thanks to God!

> *Isaiah 45:2-3 "I will go before you and level the mountains; I will break down gates of bronze and cut through bars of iron. I will give you hidden treasures, riches stored in secret places so that you may know I am the LORD, the God of Israel, who summons you by name."*

How good is our God! He goes before us to prepare the perfect path for us even by leveling the mountains and breaking down gates. All we have to do is have faith in him and walk fearless of the problems around us and keep walking to our calling in life by God.

> *Proverbs 3: 5-6 (NLT) "Trust in the LORD with all your heart and do not depend on your own understanding. Seek his will in all you do, and he will show you which path to take."*

Chapter 12

Trust God Equals No Stress

No Worries

There was a time when I got so stressed out in college that I didn't even know how I would make it through college because I had only 3 or 4 hours of sleep every day and each day was very exhausting and demanding. Every morning, I woke up with disappointments by the worries of the future and thoughts on how to make it through the day. I also was not doing really well in college and the Bible college that I wanted to go to demanded a high score, and it gave me really big worries for my future, thinking what if I don't get the scores I need to get into that university or worse, what if I even failed in college??

God even gave me a dream where, in the dream, I was in such a hurry at the train station, being so exhausted and in need of going to a particular place and I was so late. My face and body were full of sweat everywhere, and my face was already red-purple color.

Waking up with only negativities in my head every morning, the only solution and hope I had for myself was God and I asked him for help. I also asked him what the meaning of the dream was and what he wanted me to know by that dream. On that very day, while I was walking to school, l heard the Holy Spirit telling me in a calm, soft voice "You are tired because you are worried." I did not understand at first why he said that. Only after thinking for a long while, I understood completely that it was not physical tiredness that I was facing, but was mental tiredness because of all the worries I had of the future and how I was going to make it through the day.

When I got back home that day, I was encouraged to write down Bible verses on a paper, telling us not to worry and to trust in God wholeheartedly. After writing all those Bible verses down, I was prompted to close my eyes and let the holy spirit show me words to write down for myself. So it began like "don't trust," and I was already thinking in my mind like "hey, what do you mean 'don't trust'? I don't understand this at all" However, I continued writing what I saw, and it went on "yourself in your own efforts in life"(it only made sense then) and "Trust me with everything. Try your best and let it go to me".

Together it made up like this

"Don't trust in your own efforts in life. Instead, trust me with everything. Try your best and let it go to me."

It has helped me to live a very happy life without any stress at all, trusting God with everything in life. Funnily, the only bad outcomes that I had in life were when I depended only on my efforts and left God out. But, when I include God in everything, the outcome is always good. Even if it isn't, something greater always happens.

I did not realize it at that time, but I lacked faith in God as I was always worrying about everything. Now I'm living a life of fun, and I am always full of energy, waking up every day with great expectancy that God has something great in store for me every day, and I have no worries at all. In the past, when I woke up late, I used to run very fast to the bus stop from home and to college from the bus stop. When I get to the classroom in time, I was almost dying of tiredness, breathing very heavily and having some pains in the chest, feeling like my body's water contents had been sucked out completely. Now, even when I'm late for classes, I just walk slowly as usual, as God would want me to, having total peace inside and not worrying about anything at all because God is always there for us every second. When forgetting something important in the library, one would automatically have a mini panic-attack in their hearts and think like "Oh no, someone must have stolen it already! I must run back as quickly as I can so nobody will steal it". As I trust God completely with all my heart, I do not have a mini panic-attack and would only peacefully think like "Ah there's nothing to worry about at all, God's got it for me."

It may sound very illogical, but it is actually how God would like us to react to unexpected situations in life. He wants us to rely on him entirely and have no worries at all. In fact, we only usually make mistakes in life when we are fearful and full of concerns for the near future as we are not able to think carefully, and so we make bad decisions quickly. Just have complete faith in God. Give all your problems to him, rest in him and live a life full of joy.

Imagine a life where you had nothing to worry about no matter what! That is what God wants for you.

Your phone dropped? You don't worry the screen won't crack because you believe that

God won't let that happen to you. However, you still should try to catch it with your own hands in the natural world, ha-ha.

Having worries in your life is indicating a lack of faith in Jesus. Let go of all your concerns by trusting in him completely with all your problems

Psalms 55:22 "Cast your cares on the Lord, and he will sustain you; he will never allow the righteous to be shaken."

Isaiah 49:23 "You will know that I am the LORD; those who hope in me will not be disappointed."

Yes, you read that correctly, he will "never" allow the righteous to be shaken. How can he do that? It is by you, casting your cares on him. That only is your job, and it sounds challenging and illogical, but it is very easy. If you are still fearful of the future and the problems that you have in life, I encourage you to memorize just those two verses and practice releasing your cares to the LORD and have peace inside which only God can give you. Talk to him as if he is your best friend, tell him about all your troubles and ask help from him. You may think you need to go to church to personally pray or talk to God, but you don't need to go to church to speak to God. In fact, Jesus said this

Matthew 6:6 (NLT)"But when you pray, go into your room and shut the door and pray to your father who is in secret. And your father who is in secret will reward you."

Maybe you won't believe it's possible, but if you do that, I am sure you will start to see amazing results in your life when you let go of your problems to God, and you will be looking up and saying "Thank you Jesus" sooner than you think you would.

Here is just another Bible verse to ease your worries more effectively

Psalm 34:10 (NLT) *"Even strong young lions sometimes go hungry but those who trust in the LORD will lack no good thing."*

Maybe you are struggling in life now to have enough money for food and shelter. Just trust in God with everything, and you will never go hungry again! He will always provide for you, sometimes even in ways that you would never have imagined of.

Now, you may have a question for me. "What if I trusted God with something and it turned out badly? Now, what do I do? I will blame you for it."

Well friend, if something bad happened to you, even if something very disastrous happened, I encourage you to keep having faith in God no matter what because for believers, whenever something bad happens, it is always followed by something great in life even though you may not think of it. Know that God's plans for your life are so much greater compared to what you have planned for your life. Always pray for God's will to be done in your life instead of your will. Also know that whenever something happens to you when you are following God with all your heart, it is 'always' for your own good. Here is a Bible verse for it.

Romans 8:28 *"And we know that in all things God work for the good of those who love him, who have been called according to his purpose."*

His love is so deep

One day along my exciting journey with God, I was overloaded with so many tasks in life such as having about eight assignments due in 1 whole month in college and also needing to renew my passport as soon as possible. When I checked on how to renew my Burmese passport in Australia, the instructions almost made me feel dizzy as there were so many steps involved and some steps were too complicated to understand what I had to do. I was so busy the whole month, but I rested in God's promises that he would give me the grace to fulfill all my needs in life every day. I still could not find an answer on how to easily renew my passport, and because of the volume of assignments that were due that month, I didn't seem to have any time to work on it.

One day, I fell asleep during the middle of the day after class and had a dream of myself in a big brown room, sitting down on the ground, then having my eyes closed and trying to hear God's voice. There were some people around me praying for me to hear his voice, but suddenly, I sensed an evil spirit behind me and later I heard people around me gasp in fear. Then that evil spirit pulled my ear in all directions and also tried to cover it which I think it was trying to prevent me from hearing God's voice. However, it couldn't tear my ear apart, and it just disappeared suddenly. A few seconds later, I heard a very gentle, soft and clear whisper voice which was the voice of God, telling me "*My love is so deep.*"

Immediately, I woke up after hearing those gentle and peaceful words. However, I thought it was my mind playing tricks, and so I tried to search those words in the Bible but couldn't find it. So I thought it was surely my just my mind playing tricks, thinking it was a grammatical error as I thought only "My Love's so deep" is correct with the apostrophe 's'. So I just simply asked God if it was from him or not, even though I know I recognized that voice as God's voice. Immediately, I listened to the song on You-Tube 'Sinking deep' by Hillsong, and the lyrics followed "Your love so deep, is washing over me" and there's no apostrophe s there too. I was so amazed how God had answered immediately, and that the dream was from Him.

I was very pleased and even more relaxed, knowing that he keeps letting me know that he loves me and is always watching over me. I did not worry about the passport renewal issue at all as I trusted fully in him, knowing that he will help me with everything. On that night, a Burmese (my nationality) lady from Melbourne sent me a friend request on Facebook, and as usual, I accepted and asked if she knows me as I always do that to everyone who sends me a friend request on Facebook. So I asked if she knew me, and she said "no" and so I checked her profile and saw that she's a devoted Christian as well and even works at Visa Services Company in Melbourne. So I told her that God sent her to help me and explained to her about my situation. She said she could help and just asked for three simple things to renew my passport which was so easy for me as I was also so busy with all the assignment due in college that month. God is amazing! God's love is so deep! He will always supply us with everything we need for our life, and even if it is out of our reach, he will make impossible things happen for us. He will never fail us! Whatever demands you have in life, tell him and talk to him and he will always supply us with whatever we need.

Chapter 13

Power In The Name Of Jesus

This is probably the scariest chapter of my book, and it may scare you a little bit but be rest assured that there is nothing to be scared of because God made the name of Jesus above everything and God is always with us against those who are against us.

People do not realize that there is a supernatural world out there on the Earth which is impacting our natural realm. The unseen supernatural realm is so much stronger than the natural realm. We can rely on the good supernatural side to help us with our natural problems. The result is always much better than us relying on our own natural abilities in life because the power we have is nothing compared to the power of God.

While there is God and all the good angels, there's also Satan and his demons (fallen angels). There are also evil supernatural forces around us which people do not realize. The biggest mistake that people make is when they have a supernatural problem, and they rely on their own strength in the natural world to solve that supernatural problem against a demonic force while they should actually be relying on God for their solution. We are constantly caught up in a supernatural battle of good and evil where we have to get support and protection from God. When I discovered this, it's like my spiritual eyes have finally been opened to the truth as if my eyes have been blind the whole time. I felt like Harry Potter living with his uncle's family before Hagrid came to tell him he's a wizard and him finally exploring the magical world in Harry Potter's first movie.

Sadly, the most successful thing that Satan has done in this world is to make people think that he does not exist.

> *2 Corinthians 4:4 (NLT) "Satan, who is the god of this world, has blinded the minds of those who don't believe. They are unable to see the glorious light of the Good News. They don't understand this message about the glory of Christ, who is the exact likeness of God."*

I am going to tell you about the scary dreams I had of the demonic forces in the unseen supernatural realm which actually relates to my situations in real life as God gave me those dreams to show me how powerful he is against all those evil things.

Powerful Name

My sister really hates Christianity, curses at me whenever I tell her about it and always get immediately angry whenever she hears the name of Jesus as if it's a light switch to turn her angry mode on so easily. But I kept praying for her every night for her eyes to be finally be opened to the truth and to know that Jesus is all she needs for her life. I was so tired and was very discouraged to keep praying for her, and my high hopes of her getting saved were drifting away day by day. One night after praying, as usual, I had a vision of myself in the train in the middle of the desert, looking at the desert through the window. Then I saw two birds, appearing from the same left side. One was flying from my left side to the right side along a straight path but the other bird flew towards me, hitting the window and my eyes opened in reality. I had no idea what it was about, but I knew something was coming up that God wanted me to pay a good amount of attention to. I fell asleep immediately and got a dream. It was unbelievable and scary too.

In the dream, I found myself sitting in a dark basement of a house with only a dim light. Then I found my sister sitting in front of me, holding my hands while having her eyes closed. I did not know why but I had my eyes open, looking at her and I was praying in other tongues for her. While I was praying in other tongues for my sister, I suddenly felt a very evil presence around me. Immediately, my body started to become so hot as if it was burning all around everywhere. I then felt a hand grabbing my throat. It was actually a demon, but I didn't know it because I was already terrified and could not see it. I could only feel it. However, it did not try to choke me by squeezing its hand, but it pushed me back slowly while grabbing my throat. I will explain why later. As I kept resisting and continued praying in other tongues, I felt another presence of a demonic being behind me, and it grabbed the back of my shirt collar and pulled me back too! It was like as if those two demons were trying to push me backward instead of trying to kill me in the dream. My body was in so much pain already as if it was about to explode due to a huge amount of heat stored inside the body. I kept praying in tongues, bearing against all the pain and at the end, I prayed "In Jesus' name, Amen" and immediately all the demonic beings and their presence disappeared like magic and my body no longer felt any heat/ pain anymore. In the dream, my sister had no idea of what just happened, but she opened her eyes after my prayers and came to faith in Jesus. I later understood why the demons were trying to push me backward instead of trying to harm me. My sister was in front of me, and I was praying for her and so it was so clear that those demonic forces were trying to push me away from her (pushing me backward as my sister was in front of me) so that I can no longer pray for her and that she will never know Jesus. But it was only after I used the name of Jesus, they all disappeared in a blink of an eye. God also showed me in the dream that all those evil beings are so afraid of the name of Jesus and they run away from Jesus immediately. I cannot imagine myself if I had relied on my physical strength to fight against the unseen demons in the dream, surely I would have lost so miserably no matter how much I tried. This is why we should always rely on Jesus (the good supernatural side) to fight against whatever problems we have in the natural and the supernatural realm. He is always for us and never against us.

It was a very wild dream that God gave me to encourage me to keep praying for all the unbelievers to come to know that Jesus is for them and not against them.

> *Luke 10:17 "The seventy-two returned with joy and said 'Lord, even the demons submit to us in your name'"*

> *Luke 10:19 "I have given you authority to trample on snakes and scorpions and to overcome all the powers of the enemy; nothing will harm you."*

> *Mark 16:17 "And these signs will accompany those who believe: In my name they will drive out demons; they will speak in new tongues; they will pick up snakes with their hands; and when they drink deadly poison, it will not hurt them at all; they will place their hand on sick people, and they will get well"*

But of course, don't test God by drinking poison intentionally just to see if you will get sick or not. That Bible verse is written for when believers drink poison 'unknowingly.' We should never test God by willingly putting ourselves in danger.

In fact, it's written in the Bible about the time the devil tempted Jesus. The devil took Jesus onto the highest point of the temple and told him to throw himself down if he is the 'Son of God' by saying the Bible verses "He will command his angels concerning you, and they will lift you up in their hands, so that you will not strike your foot against a stone"

How did Jesus react to this?

Matthew 4:7 "Jesus answered him, "It is also written: 'Do not put the Lord your God to the test'"

This event can be found in the book of Matthew, chapter 4: 1-11

Unseen Enemies

After I had that dream of my sister, I had another dream in the next few days very surprisingly. I had a dream where I was in a very big house. I somehow found myself lying flat on the toilet floor, and it was very brightly lit. There was a woman's wig lying on the floor in front of me. It had shoulder-length hair and was black. Suddenly, it started to move by itself upwards. I didn't understand why or how at first but later I realized that it was an evil spirit trying to scare me. It wore that wig and was standing up, even though it was invisible for my eyes, I could see the wig being worn perfectly as if a real woman was wearing it, only that she's invisible whereas the wig was visible. I just knew that whatever it was, it was not something from God, so I said to it "I cast you out, in the name of Jesus" very confidently and unexpectedly, the wig fell down onto the floor flat as if someone who was wearing it magically disappeared! Again, it's apparent that whatever it was, it was so afraid of the name of Jesus and left in a blink of an eye when I used the name of Jesus to cast it out.

Another dream immediately followed where I was in the same house but in front of another room. I saw an ordinary man inside the room fighting against a demon. The man was probably around 6 feet tall, but the demon he was fighting against was about 10 or 12 feet tall, probably around twice his height. It was reptile-ish in appearance, having yellow skin with bumps/scales all over and had huge muscles. It looked a bit similar to "the Abomination" in the Hulk movie.

I saw that even though the man was trying to fight, he couldn't fight at all and the demon was torturing him again and again non-stop. Then the man was a bloody mess and was about to die. I was watching everything, and then I shouted to the demon, "I cast you out! in the name of Jesus," and immediately, the demon looked up and was screaming at the top of his voice as if he was being tortured brutally by that name.

Philippians 2:10 "That at the name of Jesus, every knee should bow, in heaven and on earth and under the earth,"

I assumed God just gave me those dreams to let me know the power in the name of Jesus. It's good to know that someone who is the most powerful in everything is on your side, always fighting for you against your enemies in life. When I was young, I always used to watch ghost or scary movies with my family and was so fearful of ghosts every night, especially when I had to walk to the toilet in the dark at night alone. It was because I only had the thoughts of defending myself by my own strength which would not have been enough. Now, however, I am not scared at all of any evil spirits trying to harm me, and I can always sleep very peacefully at night, knowing that God is always protecting me even when I am sleeping.

Psalms 121: 4 "Indeed, he who watches over Israel never slumbers or sleeps."

You may have a question like "I have read the Bible, I think God only cared about the nation of Israel because almost all the events happened in Israel and God always watched only over Israel. So how does it apply to the rest of the world?"

God's original plan since the beginning was to bring salvation upon the whole Earth by making Israel an incredibly prosperous and successful nation so the all the nations of the world would come to Israel and know about the all loving, powerful and the true God that they have. Here's a Bible verse to prove it to you.

Isaiah 49:6 (NLT) "you will do more than restore the people of Israel to me. I will make you a light to the Gentiles, and you will bring my salvation to the ends of the Earth."

The 'you' in the verses refer to the nation of Israel. 'Gentiles' refer to the non-Jews, all the people from the rest of the world.

However, when the Jews rejected the gospel after the time of Jesus, this happened. This was during the Apostle Paul's first missionary journey.

(Paul's story is incredible. He was an unbeliever, persecuting Christians and killing them everywhere but when his spiritual eyes were finally opened to the truth, he spent the rest of his life preaching the gospel across many nations that even some Christians didn't trust him at first because he had such an opposite personality towards the gospel before he was born-again. This story can be found in the book of Acts, chapter 8 and 9)

Acts 13:46-47 "Then Paul and Barnabas spoke out boldly and declared, "It was necessary that we first preach the word of God to you Jews. But since you have rejected it and judged yourselves unworthy of eternal life, we will offer it to the Gentiles. For the Lord gave us this command when he said, 'I have made you a light to the Gentiles, to bring salvation to the farthest corners of the Earth.'"

People may criticize us "Why are you spending your whole lives preaching the gospel? You should be working to become millionaires and donating your money to the Red Cross organization instead of donating it to church! Isn't that what God would want you to do? Help the poor?"

What they don't realize is that we are changing eternities for many people. To get saved and have a relationship with God, who can help them out of all their problems, like poverty, harmful addictions, and bondages and to break the chains that bind them so that they can have a brand new life which will help them become prosperous in the future because God is with them. However, we must also always help everyone in need by thinking of them as our brothers/sisters.

People may think money or fame makes everyone 'truly' happy and solves all the problems in life but there are also many people who are extremely rich, yet have a very terrible family life because they don't have the time for their family or their true hobbies due to chasing money all the time. We have also seen many celebrities committing suicide. They have fame and money just as almost everyone else in the world wants. This is because their life becomes very extremely demanding in every area of life and whatever they do is very important all the time, and many of them could not manage everything peacefully, and so they have so many worries in their life and gave up eventually as the battle every day was too much for them.

What the Holy Spirit does is balancing everything perfectly in a person's life for him to be rich, have a great family relationship and be successful in every part of their lives, by the grace of God.

> *Galatians 5: 19-25 "When you follow the desires of your sinful nature, the results are very clear: sexual immorality, impurity, lustful pleasures, idolatry, sorcery, hostility, quarreling, jealousy, parties, and other sins like these. Let me tell you again, as I have before, that anyone living that sort of life will not inherit the Kingdom of God.*
>
> *But the Holy Spirit produces this kind of fruit in our lives: love, joy, peace, patience, kindness, goodness, faithfulness, gentleness, and self-control. There is no law against these things! Those who belong to Christ Jesus have nailed the passions and desires of their sinful nature to his cross and crucified them there. Since we are living by the Spirit, let us follow the Spirit's leading in every part of our lives."*

Whatever bad addictions we have in our lives, even though we may think we will never be able to get rid of it, God can change it in an instant and delete your inner desires to continue engaging in those activities rather than you trying to control yourself from doing it. God's way is different and so much better than the ways of the world.

The way of the world will tell you to control your mind, fight against the temptation, meditate and suffer for a long while before you can fully say that you are no longer addicted to it. It works "outside in" when you control your body and suffer a long time to finally have your mind completely changed so that you won't try it again. But that method is not effective because you will always be trying to fight against the temptation to try it again.

God's way is best. When you accept Jesus as your lord and savior, the holy spirit comes into your life and changes you *"inside out,"* in a miraculous instant, you will have your mind completely changed without any efforts of your own and you will no longer desire to engage in those addictive things ever again. You will even hate to see it again because you have been baptized with the Holy Spirit and have your spiritual eyes finally opened to the truth. We have to keep reading the Bible daily and keep our eyes on Jesus instead of the temptations of the world.

Chapter 14

Supernatural Battles Everyday

Damaged Earphones Restored

I always listen to and read the Bible using the "Holy Bible" app on my IPad. One day, I was at college and was a little stressed because of all the assignments that I had coming up in a few days. I was in the noisy common room and just wanted to spend time in God's words instead of listening to the world. So, I plugged in my earphone plug into the IPad and played a chapter from the Bible. However, the sound had so many glitches every second. I was thinking "Oh man, do I have to buy another earphone now?" I kept trying so many times, but the same results occurred every single time. Finally, I somehow thought that if something is preventing me from listening to God's words, it must be the evil spirits that I cannot see with my physical eyes. So I unplugged my earphones, laid my hands over the plug and spoke confidently "Whatever evil spirits are blocking the sound and preventing me from listening to God's words, I cast you out, in Jesus' name, Amen." Then I plugged it back in and played the Bible again. Surprisingly, the sound played perfectly without even a glitch anymore!

It's amazing because I even tried about at least ten times but it only worked again perfectly when I used the name of Jesus. The name of Jesus is that powerful, even in small little thing that you think God would not care about. God cares about everything, even the little unimportant things in life. You need to have faith that your prayer will be answered, and it will be answered now or later.

You may have doubts because you may think that you only have a little faith in God. Jesus said this:

Luke 17:6 (NLT) "The Lord answered, 'If you had faith even as small as a mustard seed, you could say to this mulberry tree, 'May you be uprooted and be planted in the sea,' and it would obey you!"

The Enemy Attacks

Now I always also sometimes play chess online in my free time and my blitz rating there is around 2200-2300. One day at home, I was winning matches constructively for about even 8 or 10 matches, and my rating got up to even about 2350, and I was very happy about it. I was hungry for more so I kept on playing more matches. Unfortunately, my sister came back home and kept disturbing me non-stop for so long. I got distracted, annoyed and lost all the more matches that I played and my rating even decreased to about just below 2200, and I got angry about it inside my mind. My sister, however, kept shouting at me, and finally, I shouted at her back a bit, keeping back most of my anger inside waiting to explode. Right at that time, I was already aware that I had given in to the temptation. But I wasn't sure if it was just me, or the devil tempting me, to release my anger by exploding and smashing everything in sight. So I calmed myself down and asked God "Father, is it just my mind being annoyed and angry by itself? Or is it the devil tempting me? Help me identify what's causing me to become angry". Then I clicked on "next match" on the chess game website and very unexpectedly, my opponent's name was "root-of-evil." It was so obvious God showed me that it was the devil tempting me to burst out my anger and perform violent acts in the house.

After I won that match, I prayed for a while and went outside to the shopping mall to cool myself off. It was so noisy everywhere in public, and the only thing that was comforting me was listening to Christian songs using my earphones, blocking out the noise of the world. That was the only thing that was comforting me during my time of negative emotions. But guess what the devil did? He broke my earphones in half! The day that I really needed to listen to Christian songs was the day an earphone broke in half for the first time in my life. I was so shocked, but I managed to keep going on even though I was already so stressed. It was a terrible experience. I knew it was the devil trying to keep me away from God by making me even more angry and stressed. At the mall, I accidentally broke an egg, and everyone was watching me. It was so embarrassing. Throughout everything, I kept my faith in God and bought my sister a present as an apology, and she even apologized for her actions towards me earlier in the day. We later laughed about it. It was a wild experience. We, Christians are in a spiritual battle every day against evil forces in the world but throughout every trial in life, God is always with us, and we have nothing to be afraid of.

Know The Cause

I also had a vision one morning. In my vision, I was in a classroom somehow. Nobody saw me as if I was there as an observer but not physically there. The girls were sitting on the left side of the class while the boys were sitting on the right side, facing the girls. The teacher was teaching the class as usual. I was in the left corner at the back of the classroom. Suddenly, I saw a very dark, big and tall figure behind one of the girls and another one on the right side of the class. The one on the left said to the one on the right "Hey look, I'm going to start a fight!" and he put his mouth near the ear of a girl in the class. Then he whispered into her ear, reminding her of what her friend did to her in the past to stir up anger inside of her. Surprisingly, the quiet and shy looking girl's face got so red, and she was looking down at her book with a mad face and squeezing her fist. The demon kept whispering more lies into her ear, and she finally exploded! She jumped over her table, ran at one of the boys from the other side of the class and started fighting him. It was such a big fight that everyone in the class had to pull them both apart from each other to stop the fight.

It was just God showing me that the evil force of this world causes those things and we have to know what the real cause is which is in the supernatural realm rather than dealing with problems seen in the world. It is just like a patient in the hospital telling the doctor "It hurts when I touch my shoulder" and the doctor advising the patient "Then don't touch it" rather than trying to cure the injury.

Ephesians 6:12 "For we are not fighting against flesh-and-blood enemies, but against evil rulers and authorities of the unseen world, against mighty powers in this dark world, and against evil spirits in the heavenly places."

Don't think of Satan as a harmless cartoon character with a red suit and a pitchfork. He is very clever and powerful, and his unchanging purpose is to defeat God's plans at every turn – including His plans for your life. – Billy Graham

You may wonder "Why aren't me or my friends going through that spiritual battles like you mentioned? This is not true for us."

I love what Pastor Joseph Prince says about this question.

He said it's because you or your friends are spiritually dead! And he gave an analogy.

"Imagine you are a bird hunter in a forest. You see birds on the tree, and you shot at them. Some flew away, some died on the spot, and some got injured. Which birds do you go for first? The injured, alive ones, to make sure that they don't escape. You don't go for the dead ones because you know you can go for them anytime you want, they are dead. The devil is the hunter, and we are the birds."

I love listening to Pastor Joseph Prince's sermons.

Here's a Bible verse for supporting it.

> *1 Peter 5:8 "Be sober, be vigilant; because your adversary the devil, as a roaring lion, walketh about, seeking whom he may devour"(KJV)*
>
> *Ephesians 6:13 (NLT) "Therefore, put no every piece of God's armor so you will be able to resist the enemy in the time of evil. Then after the battle you will be standing firm."*

What is this armor of God that it is mentioned? How do I put it on to resist the devil? Please explain it to me.

I'm glad you asked. Here are the Bible verses that explains about the armor of God

> *Ephesians 6: 14-17 (NLT) "Stand your ground, putting on the belt of truth and the body armor of God's righteousness. For shoes, put on the peace that comes from the Good News so that you will be fully prepared. In addition to all of these, hold up the shield of faith to stop the fiery arrows of the devil. Put on salvation as your helmet, and take the sword of the Spirit, which is the word of God."*
>
> *But here's the good news!*

1 Peter 5:9-11 "Resist him, standing firm in the faith, because you know that the family of believers throughout the world is undergoing the same kind of sufferings. And the God of all grace, who called you to his eternal glory in Christ, after you have suffered a little while, will himself restore you and make you strong, firm and steadfast. To him be the power for ever and ever. Amen"

You may also ask or wonder "Why did God allow such a terrible thing like this to happen to me?"

God allowed us to go through trials to make us stronger in our faith through our sufferings, allowing us to see more of his power in our lives when we are helpless. Because, when we are weak, he is strong.

2 Corinthians 12: 8-10 (NLT) Three different times I begged the Lord to take it away. Each time he said, "My grace is all you need, My power works best in weakness" So now I am glad to boast about my weaknesses, so that the power of Christ can work through me. That's why I take pleasure in my weaknesses and in the insults, hardships, persecutions, and troubles that I suffer for Christ. For when I am weak, then I am strong.

Chapter 15

God's Guidance Even For Movies

As I kept reading the Bible daily, I was so fascinated by the stories in the Bible and searched on YouTube to watch movies of those events from the Bible and just Christian movies. So I found so many movies on YouTube that I wanted to watch, and I even gave a "like" to all of those movies to watch them later. Coincidentally, the next day while scrolling through Netflix, I found most of those movies there and was so happy about it. However, the only movies that I had to rent and watch on YouTube was "God's not dead" no.1 and no.2. The next day after watching all those movies, I was checking Facebook newsfeed on the bus and unexpectedly, I saw an advertisement saying "Australia! God's not Dead – A light in Darkness is nearly here!"

God's not dead no.3 was out! And was going to be shown in cinemas the next week!

I did not even search about "God's not dead" movie on Facebook or even liked any of Christian movies pages there.

The only problem was that I could not find a cinema in my town that showed that movie to watch it and also, I had nobody to watch it with as most of my friends from college were atheist. So it was Wednesday, I asked a Christian friend (Tom) to go watch it with me on Sunday, and he lived far away and told me he would get back to me about it on Saturday.

Then only I realized that I also had a very close friend, Max from the same college who was also a devoted Christian. On Thursday I had nothing to do during a free time in college and Max asked me to sit with him in the "History of Ideas" class lecture which was not in my timetable. While I was there with him, the lecturer was explaining about Christianity to all the students there, and the way he explained about the holy spirit to the students was in a way that it sounded like it's an illusion made by Christians in their minds. I saw students laughing about it, and I said to Max "The lecturer truly doesn't know about the Holy Spirit and he's explaining it to everyone like as if the Holy Spirit was an illusion. It's very sad, and that's why many people nowadays are becoming atheists as they think that God is just a figment of imagination made in our minds."

Very surprisingly, Max told me "Then you should watch 'God's not dead.' It's an excellent movie". I was so shocked because that was the first time he told me about the movie even though I had been good friends with them for many months. So I asked him "Do you know God's not dead no.3 is out already? Let's go watch it together!" It turns out, he had no idea that the movie was out already. Such perfect timings by the Holy Spirit!

But both of us did not have time to watch it as our classes finish late at night and we had to travel far from the town to watch it. The next day on Friday, Max sent me a message of a ghost movie saying "do you want to watch this tonight?" I said "of course!" as I love watching all kinds of movies.

Later that Friday night in the cinema, the trailers were showing. Sometime later, the trailer for "God's not dead no.3" was showing… but then I realized the trailer was taking so long. Then I asked Max "hey why is the trailer taking so long?" and he said, "Don't you know I bought movie tickets to God's not dead no.3?" I was extremely happy and thanked Jesus for letting me watch the movie I had wanted to see for the past week. During the movie, I was a bit worried that I would be secretly betraying Tom but later received a text from Tom saying that he can't watch the movie with me on Sunday. Such perfect timings in everything! Then only later, Max told me that only on that Friday, he saw that God's not dead no.3 was showing in the Cinema and bought the tickets immediately. What a great friend I have too!

I was so happy after watching the movie and wanted to tell everyone about the perfect timing experience that I had on those days. When I got back home after the movie, I shuffle YouTube Christian songs on on my phone. My sister came into my room and asked how my day was. I was just so happy and said: "God is good." She said "what?" I replied again "God is good" and the song from my phone came out immediately "God… is… good… all… the… time…." Perfect timing again, I laughed so loudly. It was such a great day.

Another coincidence? God's guidance!

My college chaplain, Heather was very close with me as we always organized the college church parties every Wednesday. As she went away to attend a training in Switzerland for about a month and I went back to Myanmar for some weeks, we did not meet for around two months. We talked for a long time about what we missed when we met again after two months. It was on Friday, and at the end of our conversation, she prayed for me, and I remember almost the exact words. It was like

"Holy Spirit, please guide him in everything that he does. Guide him into the college that you want him to go to. Close all the doors and only open the door you want him to go to, in Jesus' name, Amen".

Everything went normal, but as time went on, I was thinking about how I will notice when the doors are closed or when a door is opened for me by God. I knew it would be obvious. I never spoke a word about the prayer, I only "thought about it." I just told my mum that Heather and I met again after two months. We had a conversation but did not speak about it (not even about the prayer) as we always prayed when we met.

Then on Monday (3 days later), my mum sent a picture on messenger of a Christian quote! It said, "When the Holy Spirit is leading you, the wrong doors close and the right one will open."

It was almost exactly the same words that Heather prayed for me! I was very surprised when I saw the picture but just sent back a sticker, as I was busy. It's surprising because she's a Buddhist and she never even sent me any Christian quotes pictures like that before. Then I called my mum and asked where she got it, and she said "It appeared on top of my Facebook newsfeed so I thought you might like it, so I sent it to you!" and when I told her about what Heather prayed for me, she was so surprised and was already very convinced that God was guiding me. When I told my sister about it and showed her the screenshot during dinner, she was even so surprised and said "Are you serious?" out of shock.

It was already all cool and surprising, but it just makes me feel happier every-time such coincidences happen to me as I know God is always watching over me, guiding me and letting me know indirectly that he is always there for me. Remember that I never spoke a word about the prayer that Heather prayed for me before my mum sent me the picture. I only thought about the closed and open doors.

Then I remembered this Bible Verse after it happened.

> *Psalm 139:2 "You know when I sit and when I rise; you perceive my thoughts from afar."*

God is amazing!

Chapter 16

Dream Helped Friend In Need

Max and I met each other at Trinity College and have been good friends since January (nearly five months). I have never dreamt of him until one Saturday night.

In my dream, I saw him playing chess against a famous chess master in a very serious chess tournament. He was losing miserably, getting attacked and was about to lose. But then I saw him praying in other tongues (praying in the spirit / known as Glossolalia/ praying in an unknown language). When he did that, he was able to resist his opponent's attacks and his opponent was having trouble finding any other good moves to play against him. He became even more focused on the chessboard, having great difficulties defeating Max. It was evident that Max could not depend on his own strength against the enemy but could only fight against him only with prayers.

So it was 9:30 a.m. when I woke up the next day, (Sunday morning). I forgot about the dream entirely, did my morning routine and went to the Hillsong Church service at 10:45 a.m. While I was singing worship songs there, I had my eyes closed and my hands in the air, singing along with so many awesome people there, and suddenly, I remembered the dream I had the night before. I kept in my mind to tell Max about the dream that I had of him. At the end of the service, the pastor said that there would be a great message at the evening service which made me want to go to it.

Then after the service, Max texted me asking if we can go to church at night together for the night service that night. Even though I planned to study the rest of the day, I wanted to tell him about the dream, so I texted him back saying "Sure, of course, see you there."

So we attended the night service together, and at the end of the preaching, for the first time in 6 months that I've been to Hillsong Church, the pastor asked us to pray in other tongues!! All of us in Hillsong Church prayed in other tongues, and it was amazing to hear so many voices praying in an unknown language which only God can understand. Max was praying in other tongues beside me very enthusiastically and loudly which surprised me. After the service, I asked him if he had been praying in other tongues during these days and unexpectedly, he said "no". Later he opened up to me that ever since he arrived in Australia, he hadn't been praying in tongues as he had the feeling of lacking in faith and everyone in Melbourne were speaking in English which wasn't his native language, and so he got discouraged to pray in the spirit since arriving in Australia. After I told him about the dream that I had of him the night before, encouraging him to start praying in other tongues, he was very surprised and told me that he would start praying in other tongues which made me happy because I knew God had clearly given me that dream just to help out a friend keep his faith in Jesus. God is always looking out for each and every one of us all the time, and we do not have to worry about anything at all.

Now many of you may not even have heard of such thing as "praying in other tongues," it's when a believer prays in an unknown language with unknown words guided by the Holy Spirit. It's actually very amazing as it's a secret language that only the Holy Spirit prays through us to the Father. Many think it's ridiculous, but it's actually very helpful mentally and physically. The Holy Spirit prays the perfect prayers for us through us when we're praying in other tongues. For example, it may be praying for a person that I do not know or for me to avoid a car accident the next day. Here's proof of a physical health benefit of praying in the spirit.

1 Corinthians 14:4 "He who speaks in a tongue edifies himself"

"Dr. Carl Peterson, M.D. conducted a study at ORU in Tulsa, Oklahoma. Being a brain specialist, he was doing research on the relationship between the brain and praying or speaking in tongues. He found that as we pray in the Spirit or worship in the Spirit (our heavenly language), the brain releases two chemical secretions that are directed into our immune systems giving a 35 to 40 percent boost to the immune system. This promotes healing within our bodies. Amazingly, this secretion is triggered by a part of the brain that has no other apparent activity in humans and is only activated by our Spirit-led prayer and worship!" (Virkler, 2014).

It even gives 35% to 40% boost to the immune system! (Virkler, 2014).

I also think that is the reason why I now never get sick whenever I get caught in the rain, and the most I get is only a blocked nose for a day. Growing up being unhealthy, whenever I got caught in the rain, I always automatically get a blocked nose, followed by coughs and sickness the next following days!

Nowadays, even when I get completely soaked from the rain, the most I get is a blocked nose. And when I get a stuffy nose, I pray "By his stripes, I am healed"(Isaiah 53:5) and I also pray and singing in the spirit with other tongues, I get healed! It's amazing.

Language areas are in the frontal lobes, but when praying in other tongues, medical tests have found that the activity in the frontal lobes decreased and an increase in activity in the thalamus, suggesting that the language was being developed in a different way or from someplace other than the normal processing centers of speech. Believers take this as proof of the Holy Spirit praying through them (condensed -ideas from pages 200 and 201 of Born to Believe by Andrew Newberg, MD).

God speaks indirectly too!

Being very enthusiastic for God, I started volunteering at Hillsong Church in July for the night service, and as it was the first time of my life working, it was tiring for me. However, I learned so much about how the church worked and the amount of hard work involved to manage a church as I wanted to open a Church in the future. My main job was to put pamphlets on every seat and to direct people to their seats. It was really fun but tiring. So the 'next day,' my legs even hurt a little bit in the morning when I walked to the tram stop to catch my ride to college on a Monday morning at 7:30 a.m. On the tram, I listen to Pastor Joseph Prince's sermon from years back.

I was listening carefully to the sermon, and he said

"This year, God will bring you into areas where you're not comfortable. When I say uncomfortable, I mean it's uncomfortable for your flesh. God will expose you into areas where you're not strong and talented in so that you'll see his fresh supply in all these new areas."

I was like "hmm, this is relating to me a bit. I think maybe God is indirectly telling me what's going on in my life through Joseph Prince's sermon."

I continued listening, and he said

"I prophesy to you that this year, God will expose you to areas where it's not comfortable for your flesh. But it's really good for you. Because God is strengthening you."

He stopped for a while, and he continued

"It began already. Some of you had that yesterday."

I was so surprised! It was so accurate as I had just volunteered for the first time at Hillsong Church the night before. God was telling me what he's doing for me. It was amazing to know He's in control. And FYI, even the title of the sermon is "How to pray when you have no prayer" (which doesn't relate to what I heard from the sermon) from 31st August 2014, and the part I heard was from the 15th to 19th minute of the sermon.

I do not know everything, but I know one thing. Before I was a Christian, I never had such coincidences like that. But when I have a relationship with God, such coincidences happen to me almost all the time and each time, I know God is guiding me along the way.

William Temple – "When I pray, coincidences happen. When I don't, they don't."

Chapter 17

Most Unbelievable Perfect Timing Ever!

This was when I had written most of this book, and I was sharing it with my family members and some friends. I wanted God to use this book to reach out to so many other people out there who don't know that God is a loving God and has a negative view of him.

My class schedule at that time had four 8 a.m. classes which was a huge bummer for me because I had to wake up at 6 a.m. Because of this, I switched my math lecture class to another time on Monday to have more sleep for myself.

And a week passed by and it was Monday. As usual, I always prayed to God in the morning, asking him for his guidance, and to use me as a witness for Christ. I went into the new math lecture class for the first time. A Chinese girl with freckles on her face, who was my friend since the start of college sat beside me for the first time in that lecture. The first thing that I noticed about her was her freckles on her face because I had never seen an Asian who had freckles and so she was unique to me.

During the lecture, she took out her phone, showed me my own Instagram post of my "baptism" video and asked me what it was about. I explained it to her thoroughly as she does not know anything about it or even about Christianity. So I also asked her some questions about what she thinks of God and the supernatural world around us, and she sounded quite interested in talking about it. Then suddenly, I felt a need by the Holy Spirit to offer her to read my book as if the Holy

Spirit was pushing me to ask her if she would like to read my book and know about Christianity and my experience.

So I told her out of excitement, "hey, I was actually an atheist almost my whole life, and I just became a Christian last year. I have written a book about my experiences of how God gave me dreams to have a relationship with him. Would you like to read it?" Then her reply was "no, sorry, I have never read religious books before, and I probably won't understand it." I was embarrassed and in a bit of a shock because I thought that the Holy Spirit was telling me to ask her to read my book. I had the same feeling just as I had when I bought Albert the Gundam toy for him. And so I assumed it was just my feelings playing tricks on me at that time.

But then a while later, I got the same feeling inside again, the Holy Spirit pushing me to ask her to read my book. As I did not want to embarrass myself, I asked God in my mind "God if it is you telling me to ask her to read my book, please show me some obvious signs or anything that I would be aware of. I don't want to embarrass myself again." Immediately, the lecturer said we're doing an attendance quiz online and she said: "the password to open the attendance quiz is....'freckles'".

I was so shocked as it happened so immediately as if God knew everything from the start. The first thing I noticed about the girl was her freckles, the password quiz was "freckles," and it was only revealed when I asked God to show me signs to ask the girl to read my book. Then more surprisingly, there were 4 answers for the quiz, and the correct answer was "Israel." That country is the place where most of the events in the Bible occurred, and God was even known as " The God of Israel" in the Old Testament. Those two words were signs that I asked for. "Freckles" and "Israel" was enough for me to ask the girl again to read my book. We have to be sensitive to the Holy Spirit guiding us every day all the time in our lives so that we won't miss the signs and miss great chances.

So I obeyed what I assumed God asked me to do, and I (a shy guy) asked the girl again, risking embarrassment "hey, I wrote that book for people who do not know anything about Christianity so that it would be easy for them to understand when they read it. I am sure you would understand almost everything I wrote too, would you like to read it?" As expected, her reply was "ok sure then." My reaction was to look up at the ceiling saying in my mind "LORD, you are amazing. Thank you, Jesus, for using me."

So I took down her Gmail address and told her I would write a very long Email to her at night and send the written book by PDF to her, telling her not to think it's a love letter from me (my silly personality traits). So that night as I promised, I wrote a long message to her, telling her everything about the obvious signs that God gave me to ask her to read my book. She replied me a very long email starting with

"Hi, Leo,

OMG! I don't know what to say now. I was shocked when I read your email, cuz I didn't notice what you mentioned that happened in today's lecture, the 'freckles' stuff, haha."

And later saying that during the lecture, she changed her mind to read my book and that she would read it.

This is what happens when you are sensitive to the leading of the Holy Spirit. Not only will you help others, but you will also achieve such remarkable and unbelievable things in life. Just like David (in the Bible) even though he was playing the lyre in service for the king that time, his father told him to bring food to his brothers who were fighting in the war. He humbled himself and obeyed his father and did as he was told. Now, David, a teenage boy could have been full of pride and tell his father "I am already serving the king, why would I serve my brothers?" but he humbled himself and obeyed his father's instruction. He then met the 10 foot tall giant from the enemy's side, whom he defeated because he met him when he was bringing food to his brothers, who were afraid to fight against the Giant. After defeating the giant, David's name was known throughout all Israel, and he later became king. If David hadn't been humble and obeyed his father's instructions, he would not have met the Giant and never fulfilled his calling in life.

This is the same as when the Holy Spirit pushes you to be humble, such as helping the poor, doing all good godly acts and even small things that you don't think are important for you, it might as well change your life. God is good, all the time! Just do what the Holy Spirit prompts you to do.

Proverbs 22:9 "The generous will themselves be blessed, for they share their food with the poor."

Proverbs 11:17 "Those who are kind benefit themselves, but the cruel bring ruin on themselves "

Galatians 5:22-23 *"But the fruit of the Spirit is love, joy, peace, forbearance, kindness, goodness, faithfulness, gentleness, and self-control. Against such things, there is no law."*

Chapter 18

Unreliable
Scientific Assumptions

Faith in God is not based on blind faith alone, without seeing or knowing anything! There are many pieces of evidence that the Bible is 100% true, reliable and that every story in the Bible happened. The problem in the world where so many people think that God doesn't exist is because they were never taught about the evidence of the Bible in real life in schools or anywhere else and so they automatically assumed that the big bang and Evolution theory is a fact when it's just a theory. This is because schools and universities only teach them about Evolution but never from the side of creation.

According to the Bible, the Earth is just around 6000 years old, and dinosaurs and humans lived together since Adam and Eve but the atmospheric environment was completely different after the flood, and the hunting of dinosaurs by humans also led to mass extinction of the dinosaurs everywhere. This sounds crazy at first, I know. But please keep on reading.

There are so many evidences of Dinosaurs existing together at the same time with humans. People in the past would never draw pictures of or make anything concerning with dinosaurs if they had not seen one alive. Below are some examples of the pieces of evidence.

- In Acambaro, Mexico, 56 000 ceramic figures of dinosaurs were found.

- Nascu Burial Stones (300BC – 800AD) are found in Peru and over 500 of those stones showed dinosaurs. Most of them together with humans. Some of the stones had circles drawn on the side of the dinosaurs' skin. 30 years ago, fossilized dinosaur skin was found and it had circle patterns on it! People would have had to have seen a live dinosaur to draw it on the stones because the bones won't show it

- There are many cave paintings of dinosaurs on the caves everywhere in the world.

- Bricks from 12th century in Hungary were found, showing dinosaurs as well as in Germany

- The word "dinosaurs" was only invented in 1841 by Sir Richard Owen. Before then, they were known as dragons.

- Viking ships often had a dragon head (1000AD)

- Alexandar the Great reported that, when he conquered part of what is now India in 326 BC, his soldiers were scared by the great dragons that lived in caves

- In 900 A.D. an Irish writer told of an animal with iron nails on its tail and a head similar to a horse, having thick legs and strong claws. Stegosaurus had big spikes on its tail.

- Slate palette from Heirakonpolis, showing triumphs of King Nar-Mer (first pharaoh of Egypt) and long necked dragons (probably Brachiosaurs) are drawn on one of the oldest pottery found.

- Why would people put dinosaurs on their artwork if they had not seen real ones?

Marco Polo lived in China for 17 years (around 1271 A.D.) and reported that the emperor raised dragons to pull his chariots in parades. In 1611, the emperor appointed the post of a "Royal Dragon Feeder." Books even tell of Chinese families raising dragons to use their blood for medicines and highly prizing their eggs." (Creation Seminar 3- Kent Hovind- Dinosaurs).

Why would the Chinese calendar have 11 real animals and one "mythical" dragon? Most likely because there were really 12 real animals when it came to the making of the calendar.

You may ask "so how come the carbon dating of dinosaurs show that they are millions of years old?" Don't worry, I will explain it here.

- Geologic Column is a lie

- In the early 1800s, each layer of rock was given a name (like Jurassic), an age and an **index fossil.** This was done before there ever was any radiometric dating method.

- There is actually no geologic column! If there was one, it would be 100 miles deep from top to bottom.

- Scientists use index fossils to determine the age of rock layers (telling how old a layer is by the type of fossils found in the layer).

- Scientists use the rocks to date the fossils.

- That is "circular reasoning"! Scientists use fossils to date the Strata and the Strata to date the fossil.

Flaws of Carbon dating

- Carbon dating was invented in 1949.

The geologic column was where it all started. To prove that those layers are old, they picked the number as they liked and any dating method that came along had to match the geologic column, or it's rejected! Only because the geologic column had been taught for nearly 200 years now.

Scientists might have to test the sample 5/6 times until they get the number they want from the geologic column and any other results that don't match with the geologic column, they throw the results away.

Explanation of how Carbon Dating works

- The 'current' earth's atmosphere contains 0.0000765% radio-active carbon (C14)

- During photosynthesis, plants breathe in $Co2$ and make it part of their tissue. (Some of the C is C14). Animals eat plants and make it part of their bodies.

- Whatever C14 it has continues to decay.

- Half of the C14 decays every 5730 years

- Since it cannot gain anymore, it will go out of balance with the atmosphere

- So when a fossil has an an amount of C14, the scientists calculate like this

0.000765% = 0 years old
0.00003825% = 5,730 years old
0.00001912% = 11, 460 years old
0.00000965% = 17,190 years old

It all sounds good and accurate. However, there should be no more measurable C14 after 40,000 – 50,000 years.

"With their short 5700-year half-life, no carbon 14 atoms should exist in any carbon older than 250,000 years. Yet it has proven impossible to find any natural source of carbon below Ice Age strata that does not contain significant amounts of carbon 14, even though such strata are supposed to be millions or billions years old. Conventional carbon 14 laboratories have been aware of this anomaly since the early 1980s have striven to eliminate it, unable to account for it.

Lately, the world's best laboratory which has learned two decades of low- C14 measurements how not to contaminate specimen externally, under contract to a creationist, confirmed such observations for coal samples and even for a dozen diamonds, which cannot be contaminated in situ with recent carbon. These constitute that the earth is only thousands, not billions of years old." (Creation Science Fellowship, 2003).

There are assumptions that mess up everything.

It has been calculated that it would take 30,000 years for earth's atmosphere C14 to reach equilibrium. However, it has not reached equilibrium yet.

Radiocarbon is forming 28-37% faster than it is decaying.

Meaning – Earth is less than 30,000 years old, and you can't carbon-date anything.

Because you have to know when an animal lived to figure out how much C14 a dinosaur was breathing when it died.

Example

Imagine you walked into a room and see a candle burning and you're asked when it was lit.

So when was it lit?

- Measure height (7 inches e.g.)

- Measure rate of burn at which candle is melting (1"/hr)

Assumptions

- How tall was it?

- Has it always burned at the same rate?

None of these two questions' answer can be known

If you find a fossil in the dirt

The amount of C14 can be measured (length of candle) and the rate of decay (rate of burn) can be determined but that is all.

How much C14 was in it at death and has it always been decaying at the same rate? Has it been contaminated? There is no way to know these things.

Staring amount of C14 – Unknown?

Current amount of C14 - Known

Half life of C14 - Known

"When the same rock is dated by more than one method, it will often yield different ages. And when the rock is dated by more than one time by the same method, it will give different results." –John Morris, PH.D, Geology, The Geology Book, 2000, p.52

Things to consider about Carbon Dating:

- Sample of Known age – Radioisotope dating doesn't work

- Sample of unknown age – Radioisotope <u>assumed</u> to work

A few examples of wild dates by radiometric dating:

- Shells from living snails were carbon dated as being 27,000 y.o.

- Living mollusk shells were dated to be 2,300 years old.

- A freshly killed seal was carbon-dated as having died 1,300 years ago.

- One part of Vollosvitch mammoth carbon-dated at 29,500 y.o. and another part at 44,000 y.o.

Structure, metamorphism, sedimentary reworking and other complications have been considered. Radiometric dating would not have been feasible if the geologic column had not been erected first.

Molecular-clock?

It is probably the latest dating method for our species using the mutation rate of humans to date it back all the way to the beginning of the first humans. But this method also in error as this method is calculated based on considering that the 3 following factors are 100% reliable and correct.

- That humans evolved from chimps

- Radio carbon-dating as 100% reliable

- That the fossil records are accurate

- No.2 and no.3 are based on the "geologic column"(explained about earlier) which doesn't actually exist!

So when they assume all those 3 factors as true and use them in calculations, they get the dates for "mitochondrial Eve" as

- 2009 – 108,000 years old

- 2012 – 250,000–300,000 years old

- 2013 – 157,000 years old

However, when a scientist only calculated the "mitochondrial Eve" by comparing only human to human and not assuming human-chimp ancestry in 1997, the result was only 6500 years old which fits around the Biblical timeframe.

More information of this research can be found in "Answers in Genesis" website

Scientists compared Mitochondrial DNA differences in all humans and calculated the number of differences in Mitochondrial DNA that should be seen if Mitochondrial Eve lived 157,000 years ago (Nathaniel T J, 2015, p.g. 375-378).

It's calculated that if it lived 157,000 years ago, it should have around 1000 differences now as longer period of time in human history would lead to more differences. And if it lived 6000 years ago, it should have just 20 – 79 differences.

Amazingly, it's found to have only 77 differences in actual data! Meaning that the Mitochondrial Eve lived only just around 6000 years ago which fits the biblical time-frame of Adam and Eve.

This has also even been proven for many different animals as well! (Nathaniel T J, 2015, p.g. 375-378).

Is Evolution a Fact?

There are also so many reasons why Evolution is just a theory and is not based on evidence. Science only shows "Micro-evolution" which is "just adaptation changes" in a species of an animal, not from 1 kind into another kind like from reptile to birds and they assume everything came from a tiny living organism which is actually impossible. It's like telling the whole 90 mins movie by just watching 1 minute of it. Then they make people think that we all came from monkeys by showing a little animated video of a monkey slowly turning into a human and people easily believe it. However, missing links between monkeys and humans still haven't been found even today. Animated videos are just imaginations, and the fossil evidence is the ones that really count which evolutionists are still trying to find for the 'missing link.' They have been trying to find it for around 200 years already and still hasn't found it. Other so-called "missing links" such as Nebraska Man, Lucy or Java-man have already been proven to be a hoax. For example, the entire appearance of a half-monkey, half human lookalike (missing link), Nebraska Man was constructed of only a tooth found in 1922! Later, that tooth was proven to be a pig's tooth! (Scoville, 2017).

It is based on unreliable assumptions, and it just tells us how much evolutionists are willing to risk to convince that their theory is scientifically proven true when it is not. It is only a theory.

When we find 1 similar bone in a whale and a human, Evolutionists are very quick to say that we have a 'common ancestor' without any solid proof. But it just shows that we have a 'common designer' (God) who used similar structures to design us as we are all made from the dust of the ground by God. It is just mainly just a matter of perspective! It's just like having two similar lookalike pens on a table. An evolutionist would say "One pen slowly evolved into the other pen over millions of years due to the changes in the environment" They use 'millions of years' as a special ingredient to their conclusion to make everyone believe it. However, a creationist would say the two pens had a 'common designer' which is more logical to believe.

Recently around May 2018, science proved that 90% of all Earth's animals appeared at the same time by a massive genetic study of all animals! (Nicole, 2018). Finally, Science is getting closer to the truth. The more science discovers the truth, the more they will know that the Bible is 100% true and accurate.

Evolution is basically, all about living things coming from a tiny living organism to becoming big living things such as an elephant. Also about humans evolving from monkeys (small to big), there have also been so many giant human skeletons up to 12 foot tall found all over the world and it contradicts the evolution theory. We can even search on Google about it, and we can see on "worldnewsdailyreport.com" that the company, Smithsonian, admits to destructions of thousands of giant humans skeletons in the early 1900's. Just type "Giant Human Skeletons Smithsonian" on Google, and it will pop up.

It's written that "The pieces of evidence were ordered to be destroyed by high-level administrators to 'protect the mainstream chronology of human evolution at the time' according to the court ruling" (World News Daily Report, 2018).

Imagine you're the devil and people forget the history of God's creation over time, and you want to mentally downgrade all humans by lies. You would tell them "You are worth nothing, you are just an evolved monkey over the course of billions of years from a tiny organism" to let them think as if they are 'animals' with no purpose in life. And the animated videos made by evolutionists showing we evolved from monkeys, but what he won't point out the "flaws" and the "indoctrination" of evolutions by false evidence and assumptions. The devil would never tell humans "You are God's creation and you have a purpose in life."

"Our universe is made up of time, space and matter. Those three factors have to exist all together at the same time, or otherwise, it would be impossible. Suppose you have space and matter but no time, "when" you would put matter into space if you have no time?

If you have time and matter but no space, "where" would you put the matter if you had nothing to put into space?

And lastly, if you had time and space but no matter, "what" would you put into space?

So these three things have to exist together at the same time! The Bible already stated it in the first verse of the entire Bible" (Creation Seminar 1, Kent Hovind, Age of the Earth, 2005).

<u>*Genesis 1:1*</u> *"In the <u>beginning</u>, God created the <u>heaven</u> and the <u>earth</u>"*

- In the beginning = Time

- Heaven = space

- Earth = matter

Huh! It all fits, what a coincidence? Maybe the Bible is right after all!

By the way, uni = single, and verse = a single spoken sentence. Universe! Genesis 1:1?

If the Earth is also billions of years old, why do we have currently oldest living organisms that are only just around 4000- 5000 years old? We should have the oldest living organisms at least 10,000 years old if the Earth is Billions of years old.

There are also so many pieces of evidence of the biblical worldwide Flood event during the time of Noah. You can look it up by yourself, but one proof of it can surprisingly be even found in the Chinese language! Ancient China story has a very similar account of the Worldwide flood covering even the highest mountains of the Earth. Chinese language is one of the oldest languages and has been around for more than 3000 years and so when it was developed; it contained evidence of the stories that had been passed down through generations after the Flood about the Flood. For example;

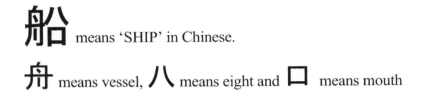

船 means 'SHIP' in Chinese.

舟 means vessel, 八 means eight and 口 means mouth

Chinese used 'mouth' to describe one person. So it means there are eight people in a vessel which make up the Chinese word 'boat.' And there were eight people in Noah's ark in the Biblical worldwide flood event. It must have really happened to even still have that evidence in the Chinese language still being used everywhere today.

I really encourage you to type on google about 'God revealed in Chinese words,' and you'll be astonished by what you'll find.

If you are interested to know so many more pieces of evidence of why the Earth isn't billions of years old, why evolution is just a bad theory and that the Earth is actually 6000 years old as the Bible says, please watch Kent Hovind's Creation Seminar series which is also available on YouTube.

Science can explain this or that by the biological study of animals, but they can never explain animal instincts such as how a newborn spider automatically know how to weave an intricate web without being taught or how a butterfly knows how to navigate a 2,500-mile route without guidance.

Only God explains that he equipped each creature with specific knowledge. Only Scripture explains animal instincts.

Chapter 19

Faith Based On Evidence

Is the Bible Reliable?

Is the Bible Reliable?

The Bible tells so many amazing stories, and almost every one of those stories has been archaeologically and historically proven to be true, especially the New Testament.

The Bible tells the story of Joseph who was the son of Jacob who was the son of Abraham. Joseph was sold into an Egyptian slavery market by his ten step-brothers, and he became Pharaoh's right-hand man, the 2nd highest position in all of Egypt, under Pharaoh. Later in his life, all his family and relatives from Syria moved into Egypt and settled there. Over some generations, the Israelites population increased, and the Pharaoh enslaved them in Egypt. But God chose Moses to help the Israelites get out of Egypt and go to the Promised Land.

There are so many archaeological pieces of evidence of that story in Egypt.

An example;

"In Egypt at the end of 12th dynasty: Syrian house appeared, the type of house found in northern Syria, the area where Abraham came from. Later, Egyptian palace was constructed on it, but occupants were not Egyptian, and that palace had courtyards, colonnades, audience chambers, belonging to a high official state.

There were 12 brothers including Joseph in total. There were 12 graves with memorial chapels on top of them in the garden behind the palace. There were 12 tribes in the Bible by names of the sons of Jacob. Palace also had a portico with 12 pillars. One of the 12 graves was very special as it was a pyramid tomb. That is extraordinary because only Pharaohs and queens of Egypt had pyramid tombs at that time. Yet! the person buried in that tomb was not a king even though he was honored with a king's burial.

Inside the tomb was a statue of a man with red hair and pale yellow skin (which is how Egyptians describe Northerners). He had a throw stick across the shoulder. Faintest remains of paint, colored stripes of a multi-colored coat can be seen at the back of his shoulder. That matches exactly with the story of Joseph in the Bible. The Multicolored coat is a gift that his father gave him, meaning he was the favorite of his father" (Patterns of Evidence: Exodus, 2014).

There aren't any other statues of a Semite of this kind in Egypt.

More about the archaeological findings and evidences of the Joseph / Moses / Joshua stories in the Bible are documented in the documentary film "Patterns of Evidence: Exodus" which presents so many more evidences and is also available on Netflix.

-There are over 2000 "specific" prophecies in the Bible which have already been fulfilled. There are no such prophecies in the 'scripture' of any other religion. It also can't be said that those prophecies were written after the events took place as many of the events only happened hundreds or thousands of years after the prophecy was made and those prophecies are very highly specific in detail so it's not something loose that can be criticized. The Bible is 100% accurate and reliable!

There are over 300 prophecies alone about Jesus which he fulfilled every one of them, clearly showing that he was the Savior that the Old Testament wrote about. Our brains are very knowledge-limited, and we will always usually make bad decisions whenever we use our knowledge-limited brains to make big decisions so we should always rely on something that is 100% reliable and accurate to guide us in our life.

God's knowledge is unlimited! And the Bible is his written word book for us to get to know him and have a daily relationship with him. God can give us wisdom if we simply ask for it from him so that we can use it to make good decisions in important matters. Human wisdom tends to make mistakes even though if it is really good, it's not 100% reliable.

I do not want to offend anyone reading this, but I believe all other "Holy Scriptures" from other religions came from human wisdom as they are not 100% reliable or accurate. Here's a great example.

"The Muslim Koran says that Allah created the Earth flat, and the Hindu scriptures describe the Earth not only as a flat triangle but as held up by giant elephants who are standing on the backs of giant turtles in a giant pool. The Buddhist Scriptures even gives us the names of the elephants. Mahapadina holds up the world in the South. However, the Bible just didn't say the Earth was just round but also that it's suspended in space" (Medley, 2013, pg.32).

I think the difference of the results between human wisdom and God's wisdom is apparent.

Colossians 2: 3-4, 8 "In him lie hidden all the treasures of wisdom and knowledge. I am telling you this so no one will deceive you with well-crafted arguments. Don't let anyone capture you with empty philosophies and high-sounding nonsense that come from human thinking and from the spiritual powers of this world, rather than from Christ."

Reliability of the New Testament

History classes in schools and colleges teach about Caesar, Plato, Thucydies and Herodotus all the time and never about the Bible, especially the New Testament even though it's a more reliable work than all those four historian figures!

Don't believe me? Check this out for yourself!

WORK	WRITTEN	EARLIEST	TIME-SPAN	# of COPIES
Caesar	100 - 44BC	AD900	1,000 yrs	10
Plato	427 - 347BC	AD900	1,200 yrs	7
Thcydides	460 - 440 BC	AD900	1,300 yrs	8
Herodotus	480 - 400BC	AD900	1,300 yrs	8
New Testament	AD40 -100	AD125	25 yrs	24,000 (5000 Greek)

(Medley, 1996, pg.26)
Scholars test the accuracy of the works by

- Shorter time span between witness's timeline and oldest writing
- Larger number of manuscripts

Clearly, the New Testament is the most reliable one (Medley, 2013, pg.26).

New Testament is not the only historical document from 1st century referring to Jesus! There were even non-Christians and anti-Christian writers during that time including Roman and Jewish historians who wrote about Jesus.

"There is more historical evidence for Jesus Christ than for any other historical person. There are literacy works from his friends and foe, archaeological evidence, letters, correspondence, and historians" – Researcher Robert Morey

A complete manuscript of Isaiah (oldest book in the Bible) was discovered in 1947. An ancient book that claims to be the inspired word of God is also the book that survives with content intact (Medley, 2013, pg.27).

Everyone believes in Alexander The Great and even historians consider the documents of him as trustworthy even though he died in 323 B.C. and his two earliest biographies were only written '400 years' after his death which is nothing compared to the reliability of the New Testament (Strobel, 2013, pg. 33).

Did Jesus Rise From Death?

There's more proof that Jesus rose from the dead after three days than any other fact in Roman History!

Some say that Jesus didn't die but was laid unconscious in the tomb for three days. However, it's impossible because the professional executioner's job was to kill Jesus and he would have been killed if Jesus didn't die. Moreover, he even pierced a spear through Jesus' side, resulting in blood and water flowing out of the body which Science confirms that those details are evidence of a dead body (Medley, 2013, pg.21)

In spite of this, the Romans were even aware of the prophecy that Jesus would rise from the dead after 3 days and so, even some soldiers were appointed to guard the tomb, making sure that nobody would come and steal the body to make it look like Jesus rose from the dead because of the empty tomb. Yet, it's written that an angel appeared and made the guard so frightened that they ran away from the tomb and Jesus rose from the dead.

It's also a fact that the empty tomb has never been explained except by Jesus rising from the dead.

There were over 500 eyewitnesses of the resurrected Jesus on one occasion. Even almost all of Jesus' disciples died by the hands of the Romans, acknowledging that Jesus rose from the dead, not even denying one time that they did not see the resurrected Jesus. Nobody would ever die for a cause that they know is not true.

Charles Colson became a Christian after being put to prison when the "Watergate" lie was exposed. He compared "Watergate" and resurrection" events and knew that his men didn't even keep the lie going by lying for a few weeks and knowing surely that none of them would have gone to their deaths like the disciples in the resurrection event (Medley, 2013, pg.23).

Here is another big evidence. The Jesus movement was getting crazier, so the Romans killed the leader of the movement, Jesus, to stop the movement but the movement even grew so much bigger and faster as so many people claimed that they saw the resurrected Jesus. Many religions or cults usually die out when the religious leader dies, but it was the opposite for Christianity when Jesus died.

Paul was a Roman citizen with high status. During the time when people were running around spreading the news about seeing the resurrected Jesus, he hated them so much that he persecuted so many Christians, putting most of them to Jail and even killing them. After an encounter with the resurrected Jesus one day, Paul became a Christian and preached about Jesus to so many people around the world, and it was so amazing yet unbelievable that many believers even doubted him as he was killing most Christians before. Paul was later caught by the Romans, and when asked to testify that Jesus did not rise from the dead, he denied by even willingly giving away his own life to testify to what he believed was the truth: that Jesus rose from the dead.

"In any unbiased courtroom in the world, if the evidence for the resurrection of Christ were presented, it would be adjudged to be an absolute historical fact!" – Dr. Simon Greenleaf of Harvard

When we consider those many pieces of evidence carefully, we can fully be rest-assured that Jesus rose from the dead. Jesus didn't just rise from the dead spiritually, floating like Caspar, the friendly ghost. He had a real body made of flesh and bones just like us. But he could transcend matter as time no longer had any impact on him. He was no longer affected by time, and so he could appear here, disappear suddenly and appear 100 miles away. And believers of Jesus will all have a body like him after death. He conquered death for us as we all are afraid of death to venture into the unknown world.

So if you are an unbeliever, please think of this. Imagine you declare out your own opinion of the afterlife by the knowledge-limited mind you have and tell everyone that there is no afterlife or that the Bible is not true. Whereas, the Bible has been proven to be 100% accurate and true including all the 2000 specific prophecies has been fulfilled. Now imagine you are not yourself and you're someone else, where would you put your faith in? Would you put your faith in the Bible or in what a person says by his/her own very knowledge-limited mind?

Chapter 20

Knowing Someone Personally

If you want to know about a person without talking to him directly, what his personality is like? Is he patient or short-tempered? Is he a lunatic? Or is he a good man? Who would you ask to know more about that person?

Would you ask a complete stranger about him or his best friend who knows almost everything about him and has a relationship with him? Clearly, you would ask someone who loves him, has a relationship with him and knows all about him. Just as people would want to know about the true personality and the intention of a criminal when caught, they wouldn't ask the police about the criminal as what all the policemen would know are only the records of the criminal, nothing more. This is why in investigations, FBI agents in movies always visit the family, relatives or close friends of the criminal to ask about him as they are the ones who truly know him, his personality and his true intentions. They are the most reliable ones to ask too as they have a personal relationship with him.

You wouldn't ask anyone who is a stranger to him and doesn't have a relationship with him, even though he may know much about the person's personal records, he'll never know that person's real personality and mind. It's just stupid to do that. It's just as you wouldn't ask your friends about your mother's personality because only you know your mum personally and has a relationship with her. Only people who have a personal relationship with a person can tell the truth about the person's personality.

This sounds very clear and obvious at first as if even a little kid can understand it but actually, people make mistakes in real life about God just the same way. They listen to what unbelievers say negatively about God and think it's true. Just like Atheist/Anti-Christ pages on FaceBook, how many people there do you think have a relationship with God? Most likely none! They are just criticizing and mocking someone whom they don't know personally. Those unbelievers don't even know God personally!

So if you want to know about God and what he is like, please ask from someone who loves God and has a personal relationship with him instead of asking someone who doesn't even know him truly. Unbelievers may know much about the Bible, they may have read the whole book over 20 times, studied it carefully for many years but! They don't have a relationship with God, and that's what matters the most when you want to know someone. They are just like police officers who have carefully analyzed the crimes and personal records of a person, but they don't have a relationship with the person, and so they don't know his heart personally. Talk to passionate believers if you want to know about Jesus! Don't talk to unbelievers about God, all you will hear are narrow-minded opinions about a person they are not even friends with.

God says

"I have been misrepresented by those who don't know me" (John 8:41-44)

It's really sad when we think about it.

Chapter 21

Love Never Fails

If you happen to have bitterness or anger towards someone for what they did badly to you in the past, you may want revenge against them, and it is a very evil thing to want to hurt someone. Only more negative events will come out of negative thoughts.

People say "fight fire with fire," but I say

Fight fire with "water" which is love.

Even though the fire may be looking disastrous now, an unlimited supply of water over time will always put out the fire. In any bad relationships with anyone that you may have right now, whatever you do concerning with that damaged relationship with anyone, doing anything that is not of "love" will only lead to more problems in the future. So why do you keep creating problems for that damaged relationship that you value with anyone by complaining? This is just pure "foolishness" to fight fire with fire with the aim to extinguish the fire because it will only cause a bigger fire.

You want people to understand you, know their faults and apologize to you first (this is ego) when you yourself are blind to your own faults. This is just the same as two blind men walking and falling into a hole. Open your own eyes first before trying to open the eyes of others. And without love and forgiveness, you yourself are completely blind to the simple solution to the problem.

Matthew 7:3 "Why do you look at that speck of sawdust in your brother's eye and pay no attention to the plank in your own eye?"

You will only hurt the other person more if you try to remove it yourself because you cannot remove it properly as you are blind to the truth of LOVE.

What we all really want in our hearts is to have love with one another everywhere all the time.

- You may think you are right and the other person is wrong, and so you may not want to humble yourself and say sorry. Meanwhile, the other person is thinking he/she is right just the same way as you do.

- Never think of yourself as the "righteous" one in the situation. This is just plain foolishness. Because WE ALL have our faults no matter how small or big it is that caused the fire to break out in the first place. We have to be humble and apologize to the other person first for whatever we had done (even for things we do not know of) to them. Admit your faults humbly if you really treasure that relationship that you have with whomever you loved.

People also say "If someone treats you badly, kick him/her out of your life and live peacefully."

But this is not the correct way. The people who mistreated you with hate are the ones who need you. This is because they have a disease that requires a cure! You need to help them! The only way to cure such a disease is by the medicine of "Love." Offer/give that medicine to them every day! Once they taste it and know that it is sweet, they will take it every day, and they will be full of love overtime! It will come back to you and spread to others too.

The effect may not happen overnight, but over time, the disease will surely disappear one day. Why would you ignore a homeless person when you have so much money in your pockets? In the same way, you have LOVE which can cure bitterness that the other person has in their hearts. Use it! Use love! Never waste true love! It's a precious free gift inside us that God has given us which can never be bought with money. Bless others with love no matter what they did to you.

Never condemn the other person by just blaming them for everything wrong that they did or are doing. Instead, HELP them by showing them how it should be done the right way with love and always treating them with 100% love all the time.

Be humble and apologize or forgive first. No matter how high your position in life is. Do it no matter how right you think you are! There always had to be a reason for the person to hate you in the first place. Don't have such a big ego. It only causes blindness to LOVE which is the only solution.

So how do you get this "LOVE" if you don't have it inside you? Draw as much love as you want from Jesus who can offer you an unlimited amount of love that can even make you cry. So as God still forgives and loves you all the time even though you may have hurt him by cursing his name or anything else, you can easily do the same for others as your heavenly father has done for you once you know his love for you.

Fill people with LOVE. Don't throw them away!

1 Corinthians 13:8 "Love never fails."

1 Corinthians 13:4-7 "Love is patient, love is kind. It does not envy, it does not boast, it is not proud. It does not dishonor others, it is not self-seeking, it is not easily angered, it keeps no records of wrongs. Love does not delight in evil but rejoices in the truth. It always protects, always trusts, always hopes, always perseveres."

1 John 4:8 "God is love."

Those are the true qualities of what God is like towards all of us; don't let anyone tell you God is impatient or not loving. God is love, and so if you spend more time with God, you'll have so much love and grace inside of you that you're going to start loving everyone who you even hated so much before and it will change your life.

Matthew 5:43-44 "You have heard that it was said, 'Love your neighbor and hate your enemy.' But I tell you, love your enemies and pray for those who persecute you."

Matthew 5:46 "If you love those who love you, what reward will you get? Are not even the tax collectors doing that?"

Chapter 22

God Loves Everyone

Does God Love Homosexual People?

As this chapter is about God's love, you may also question me about God's view towards homosexuality. Does God love homosexual people? The answer is YES. This is because God loves us no matter what in spite of all our sins.

According to the Bible, homosexuality is a sin, yes. However, lying is a sin as well! And we can admit that we all are lying almost all the time. A white lie is no different. It's still a lie. Just because a person is straight and the other person is homosexual, it does not make one better than the other because in God's eye, we 'all' are of sinful nature and nobody is better than anyone else. However, even when we are all full of sin, Jesus died for us out of love. What does this mean? This means God loves you and has done everything he can to embrace you with his love even when you're a liar, even when you're a thief, even when you're a sick psychopath.

Romans 5:8 "But God demonstrates his own love for us in this: While we were still sinners, Christ died for us."

This means even when you're a homosexual person, Jesus died for you out of pure love to embrace you with his love and grace.

This means even when you're at your worst and most disgusting state of mind, Jesus still died for you out of pure love, even knowing that you might never love him back. That is the highest form of love that ever exists which only comes from God.

Can a homosexual person go to heaven by accepting Jesus? Answer is YES!

It's the same question as "can a liar get saved?" Even after we've made Jesus our Lord and Savior, we would still lie here and there sometimes but Jesus had died for all of our sins: past, present, and future! No matter what we do, we'll get saved after accepting Jesus.

This is because if you didn't do any kind of works to get saved, it doesn't depend on your works to lose your salvation too.

Ephesians 2:8-9 "For it is by grace you have been saved, through faith – and this is not from yourselves, it is the gift of God – not by works so that no one can boast."

So does this 'amazing grace' of God give people license to sin or still engage in a sinful lifestyle? No, it is actually the opposite because it will only give power to people to change their ways when they are 'born-again' as their hearts are changed by the Spirit of God working inside them for themselves to change their ways to be more like Christ every-day. Our job to only accept Jesus and let the Holy Spirit take over our life and change us.

He Reaches Out To Everyone

As you've already read how much God tries to reach out to everyone through me and how he has been guiding me throughout my life, here's another event where God showed me a bit like a warning in the dream of the future, and he worked his way for it through me.

It was on an exam day, just a few days before I leave Australia to go back home for a two weeks mid-semester holiday. I woke up around early in the morning, very frightened because of a dream I had. In the dream, I was at a classroom in college, and the class was going along, as usual, nothing special. But as the class finished, I stepped out of the classroom, and I was suddenly teleported into my grandparents' home back in Myanmar. I walked around the house and went into the bedroom where I saw my uncle lying on the bed, breathing in and out violently in a weakened state as if he was about to die anytime soon. Then I saw my grandparents standing around the bed he was on, and they leaned over towards him.

Moreover, I saw the most extraordinary thing I've ever seen in a dream. I saw a pale white figure come out of each of their bodies and they were hugging each other in mid-air between the three physical bodies. I was standing there watching the whole event happen and was crying very passionately as I knew he wasn't a believer and I knew that I could not save him. While I had my eyes closed and was crying, someone's hand held my hand and squeezed it very tightly, and I opened my eyes to find out that it's my uncle's hand that was stretched out from his deathbed, holding onto me. It was as if he used the last strength he had in his body to hold my hand and tell something by squeezing my hand as if he was trying to ask for help.

And so I woke up being frightened, thinking something terrible might happen to my uncle. I prayed for God to tell me what to do and I started using my phone, saw a YouTube video preaching video about "fasting" and that miracles come out of it when we fast as we concentrate more on Jesus and less of us and our daily needs. And so as I thought I needed to fast for somehow helping my uncle, I fasted that day for him even though my whole family criticized me so much for it, saying that I'm so stupid to believe such things, but I obeyed God rather than men. It was a very lonely and unfortunate experience to go alone against your family who doesn't understand why you're doing it. I thought if I didn't act in this manner, my uncle would be in danger, so I had to try everything I could as if I had no choice because I loved him very much. I successfully did fasting on that day, praying to God for protecting us against whatever negative is to come in the future. I even thought I was going to be crazy as my whole family spoke badly of me and told me I was becoming crazy but I assumed that it was only the devil trying to tempt me into breaking my fast that day.

I never told my family about the dream I had but I only requested my mum that we visit grandparents' home, secretly hoping to see my uncle once I arrived in Myanmar on Friday. We did visit my grandparents' home immediately after I landed in Myanmar, but unfortunately, my uncle was not there. On Saturday, I hung out with my friends which you will read about an amazing thing that happened that day in the next chapter. Then on Sunday, very surprisingly, my uncle visited my home! It was surprising because he only visits my home rarely about only 1 or 2 times a year. He arrived at 11 a.m. that day with his friend and just planned to have lunch with my family and leave around 1 p.m. for attending a ceremony at a hotel around 2 p.m. I prayed that morning asking God to use me to reach out to him if that is his will for that day. So after having lunch around noon, my uncle asked me some questions about Christianity, and I explained very carefully and patiently to him. He was interested to know everything about Christianity, and he was open-minded and wise. I realized that he was starving to know the truth about everything and so we ended up just sitting down at the table and just talking about God for 4 hours straight!. He even decided not to attend the ceremony at the hotel anymore just to talk more with me about Christianity. It was tiring for me, but I enjoyed every second of explaining it to him about God for 4 hours. After the conversation, he told me he's very interested in knowing even more about God. He even said he'll even start reading the Bible and watch Christian movies. Only then I told him about the dream that I had, that I had been praying for him and that my prayers had been answered as it was clear that he was very eager to know the truth and I've told and explained much about it to him. After I told him about the dream, he confirmed me that my dream is really true as he is a single man living with my grandparent, saying that the only people whom he loves the most are his parents!, hence why I dreamt of the grandparents hugging him on his deathbed instead of all other people. It's amazing! How God always reach out to people who long to know the truth about him!

I honestly believe you have this book in your hands because God is reaching out to you through this book.

Don't have a hardened-heart

My holiday back home wasn't really like a holiday for me as I was telling everyone about Jesus and having very long conversations with everyone about God. Most of the people were open-minded, and so they learned so much more about what they never knew anything about. But some were very narrow-minded and only stuck to what they knew about Buddhism as almost everyone I know in Myanmar are Buddhists. There was a friend whom also asked me many things about Christianity and we had a discussion for such a long time, and he followed me along on the car to a mall to meet other friends. The chauffeur and I are very close as we have known each other for over ten years. Along the way, we talked about Jesus Christ, and even though I had told the chauffeur and my friend about Jesus Christ, they kept insisting and declaring that Buddha is the true God and that Jesus was just only an ordinary man and not the son of God (which is ridiculous). I was very annoyed because even Buddha himself refused to be called "God" by his followers. What was even worse is that they claimed that Jesus was a Buddhist monk before he started performing miracles at age 30. It was the most annoying thing I've ever heard because it's written in the Bible that he was a carpenter (he lived like a normal human like us). He was the Son of God. He didn't need to seek enlightenment as "he was the enlightenment" whom people went to to get the true meaning of life. So when I asked them "So if he was a Buddhist monk, why didn't he preach about Buddhism teachings when he started preaching? He only preached about God and the kingdom of heaven," and they answered very stubbornly "He preached about Buddhism teachings and that's why he was killed! Buddha told him not to go preach there, but he didn't listen." Oh, you can already imagine how annoyed I was! So I tried to correct them by explaining to them very patiently that it is not true and that the Bible clearly said Jesus preached about God (not Buddhism teachings), knew he was going to be killed before he even went to Jerusalem and he did it to save everyone. But no, they kept declaring out their opinions and everything they think of against the Bible, even saying that "The Bible is just a worthless book written by many crazy idiots." And as I knew they were too stubborn and not open-minded like other people to be corrected, I stopped arguing with them and just stayed silent, letting them keep declaring their knowledge-limited opinions against the Bible and Jesus as I remembered these verses.

> *Matthew 10:12-14 "When you enter the home, give it your blessing. If it turns out to be a worthy home, let your blessing stand; if it is not, take back the blessing. If any household or town refuses to welcome you or listen to your message, shake its dust from your feet as you leave."*

> *John 9:39 "Jesus said, "For judgement I came into this world that those who do not see may see, and those who see may become blind."*

Meaning that those who are humble enough to admit that they don't know everything with their own knowledge-limited minds and depend on the Bible as a source for their life, they may finally see! But those who claim that they know everything about everything in the universe would think they know the truth when actually they don't, and they reject the Bible as a source of knowledge and guidance, so they become blind to the truth and the true meaning of life.

During the flight back on the plane, I was reflecting on my holiday about everything. I was delighted that my friend Tommy got saved (written in the next chapter) and that everyone knew about Jesus. However, I was still very annoyed, and I'll call it "disturbed" by what happened on the car with my friend and chauffeur. I was feeling despondent for them as they're too stubborn to know the truth and so I asked God what to do about it. Then I opened my Bible and immediately, these Bible verses spoke out to me that I even highlighted it.

> *Proverbs 9:7-9 "Whoever corrects a mocker invites insults; whoever rebukes the wicked incurs abuse. Do not rebuke mockers or they will hate you; rebuke the wise, and they will be wiser still; teach the righteous, and they will add to their learning."*

It spoke out to me so strongly and touched my heart about how true it was.

Then I realized that believers could never argue facts or knowledge about Jesus with an unbeliever to convince him/her enough to convert her as only those who are born again can see the kingdom of God (John 3:3). It is as if when a believer and an unbeliever are in a room together and there is an object which a believer can see but the unbeliever cannot see as they're not born-again. No matter how much they argue, the unbeliever will never be able to see the object due to their hardened hearts to the truth of the gospel. They will only be able to see it when they become humble and low-in spirit and let Jesus take over them which I am praying for. I am trying to make you see the object that I see.

God is always out there to guide you in everything that you do!

However, be careful of people who use only 1 Bible verse to claim something which is actually a false statement as they don't study the Bible carefully. For example;

> *Mark 11:24 "Therefore I tell you, whatever you ask in prayer, believe that you have received it, and it will be yours."*

Now many people would say you can ask anything that you want even for bad things! But this is because they don't study the scriptures carefully. So once everyone asks God for selfish things and doesn't receive it, they don't believe in him anymore. However, God hides secrets for those who seek him with all their hearts. Here's the other verse that needs to be known in order to understand why Mark 11:24 didn't work.

> *James 4:3 "When you ask, you do not receive, because you ask with wrong motives, that you may spend what you get on your pleasures."*

Big revelation for some people out there!

It's always best to let the Bible interpret itself (scripture for scripture) for you instead of you declaring your opinion on it as it would most likely produce unsatisfactory results.

Here's another example;

> *Matthew 7:21 "Not everyone who says to me, 'Lord, Lord,' will enter the kingdom of heaven but only the one who does the will of my Father who is in heaven."*

So many people frighten other people by telling them that they are not "good enough" to enter heaven based on their good works and they will never tell them the will of the Father. But we are not saved by works but by grace through faith. The "Lord, Lord" in the verse means for people who don't accept "Jesus" but only God which is not enough. And this is the will of the Father.

> *John 6:40 "And this is the will of him that sent me, that every one which sees the Son, and believes on him, may have everlasting life." (KJV)*

Our good works do not save us. If our works save us, we will never enter into heaven because we all have sinned at some point and our good works cannot save us. We only need to believe in Jesus, and we are saved by faith in him. Here are the Bible verses to prove it.

> *Ephesians 2:8-9 "For it is by grace you are saved through faith - and this is not from yourselves, it is the gift of God —not by works, so that no one can boast."*

Here's another one just for you to be even surer of your salvation through faith in Jesus.

> *2 Timothy 1:9 "He has saved us and called us to a holy life-not because of anything we have done but because of his own purpose and grace. This grace was given us in Christ Jesus before the beginning of time."*

Chapter 23

An Unbelievable Salvation Story

God loves those who hate him, those who use Jesus' name in vain. In spite of those things, God is always trying to have relationships with them. Why? Because God loves us like any father love's his children. No matter what they have done, a father would do anything he can to save their child's life when they are in danger. Here's is a story of how God saved an atheist who wanted nothing to do with God and always shared posts on Facebook that makes fun of God. God's love is never-ending towards us! This is why Paul said, ***"Here is a trustworthy saying that deserves full acceptance: Christ Jesus came into the world to save sinners – of whom I am the worst" (1 Timothy 1:15).***

> ***Roman 5:8 (NLT) "But God showed his great love for us by sending Christ to die for us while we were still sinners."***

If you want someone who loves you to the full extent with unlimited love and forgiveness, someone died to save you and that someone is now presently more alive and powerful than ever to help you with everything in your life! Jesus Christ is always there for you! It's your own choice to push him away or to let him into your heart and change your life.

So here's the story of the atheist friend that I was talking about!

My best friend Tommy had always been chatting with me on Facebook every day even though we are on the opposite side of the world from each other. He was a devout atheist, and I was a very devoted Christian, so we always talked about God and had so many discussions together. As he was my best friend, I've always told him every bit of my experience with God, and yet, he still said it happened out of chances that I dreamt the right dream at the right time and still didn't believe in God. He even liked some atheist pages on Facebook and always shared posts that criticize or makes fun of God. I've always told him to give Jesus a chance and see the results, but he never did. He even told me he got a dream once. In the dream, he and I were at a restaurant, and the noodle bowl was served for each of us. While eating, the waiter came to us, asked if he could try my soup and I let him. After he tried the soup, he was so amazed and loved it so much that he drank all of it instead of giving it back to me. That dream was really interesting as I believe God gave it to him to encourage Tommy to give Jesus a chance, instead of pushing him away all the time. At one point, he even said "I want to declare this to you. I'm sorry. But I want to spread atheism." That broke my heart as I wanted everyone to have a relationship with God.

He never believed that dreams had meanings. But one thing I loved about him was him being very open-minded about everything and being so humble. I thought there was no hope for him. The worst scenario I imagined in my head was me telling him about Jesus on his deathbed and him finally accepting Jesus when we're so old and about to die. However, I had always been praying to God for his hardened heart to be softened and for God to open his spiritual eyes to the truth.

My parents visited me in Australia, and I sent presents for my best friends Tommy and Kris through my parents. However, when they got back home, they wrongly delivered the presents to the wrong addresses, and so Kris got Tommy's presents, and Tommy got Kris' presents. Even though I wanted them to receive the correct presents, I assumed it was God's hands working in this, so I just prayed about it and trusted in Him. I put some Christian stuff in there too like a little Bible and the Father's Love Letter with hopes of him giving a chance for God. Tommy and Kris planned to meet each other and exchange the presents but Tommy never could as a big shock happened to his family in April just after I sent the gifts.

So one day in late April, shockingly, Tommy lost his 20 years old brother to a gun accident in the USA while he was still in Myanmar and it was a big shock for every one of us as he was such a good and loving friend to everyone around him. That happened around April 2018, and he got into a deep depression. He only still chatted with me through Messenger, telling me about his depression and all his problems in the family due to the sudden, devastating, shocking accident. As I always found happiness in Jesus as a Christian even in my dark times, I pointed him to Jesus whenever I could, but he still denied the offer. I kept praying for God to heal his hollow wound and asked God to be with him during his troubled times and keep reaching out to him. I knew it was evil forces that caused his brother to die out of accidental gunshot but I never really understood why God would let it happen to his brother, however, over time I did. I just kept telling Tommy "One day you'll understand why God let it happen" as I trusted in God 100% and knew there always had to be a good reason for everything that happened.

A few weeks after losing his brother, Tommy told me that he and his family had dreamt about his brother almost every night. Tommy said his brother even spoke to him directly in the dream. He said that he had a long conversation with him in the dream about everything that had happened. He started taking detailed notes on all the dreams he had every day. Finally, his hardened heart began to soften as he realized that there are supernatural forces around us all the time. He still did not believe in God, but he knew something was going on in the spirit. I always thought his brother was an unbeliever. But then he told me that his brother was, in fact, a true believer who went to church and wanted to be a Christian. That was when I finally understood why God let the tragic events happen. His brother died in a very weak state. But now he is alive, young, handsome and energetic in heaven! We should feel happy for him! If we have a sad feeling, it is for ourselves!

In early June, I bought flight tickets to return home during my two weeks mid-semester holiday (from 22nd June to 7th of July). I never told Tommy anything about it as I planned to surprise him when I got back home. Just a few days after I bought the flight tickets, Tommy told me he had a dream, and by the dream, somehow he knew that something so special was going to happen to him just around the last week of June! Only then I told him I had a surprise for him and sent him the pictures of my flight ticket details and he was so happy and surprised! We hung out at the mall with Kris the whole day on 23rd of June (1 day after I got back home) and both of them finally exchanged the presents that I had given them. Tommy and I had dinner there after Kris left and we talked about so many things as we're very close friends. We even talked about God, but that time, he was very eager to know about those things, and so we talked such a long time about it. When we each got back home, he sent me a picture of a page of the green little Bible where it says "For God so loved the world that he gave his one and only son, so that whoever believes in him will not perish but have everlasting life"(John 3:16) in Chinese language, saying that it's a beautiful saying. I thought he was joking or mocking, but it turned out that he was touched by it. He then went on to tell me about a memory of his childhood relating to that verse.

When he was a kid, he used to pray to God before eating as his Christian Uncle taught him to and his uncle also taught him so many things about God / The Bible and especially taught him John 3:16! Unfortunately, his uncle passed away, and he forgot what the scripture and verse was. Even though he tried to find his Uncle's Bible in hopes of being able to find the verse again, all his uncle's belongings, including the Bible were burned as a family tradition and he was sad about it. Later on in life, he forgot everything about God and became a stubborn atheist. And now he found that verse again and was touched by it.

He also finally checked all the presents I gave him and said he felt so "blessed" after reading the Father's Love Letter that I put into the present. Minutes later, he said again "Today I feel so blessed" and within seconds, "I think I'm into this." God answered my prayers that day! And Tommy, from being a hardcore atheist, became a believer that day. God reached out to him when he was hurting, and he received God's grace and love. He went on texting me "I'll now leave the Atheist Republic Facebook Group and dislike the page. I just did it". The transformation was so quick as if it happened in the blink of an eye!

Only on that day, I understood why God made my parents give the presents to the wrong address in the first place so that he could use my gift for Tommy to reach out to him when he needs God the most at his darkest times. God is always out there for you. You need to receive him into your heart. And Tommy's dream that something special was going to happen at the last week of June came true as on the 28th of June (during last week of June), I had the pleasure of visiting his home and personally leading him into the salvation prayer for accepting Jesus as our Lord and savior! God is so kind for allowing me to personally lead him into the salvation prayer as he knew I always wanted to do that instead of letting Tommy become a Christian himself alone as I did when I accepted Jesus alone in my room on my bed.

Ezekiel 34:11 "For this is what the Sovereign LORD says: I myself will search for my sheep and look after them."

Jesus Christ is the good shepherd, and we are the sheep. Even though most shepherds wouldn't care if 1 out of 100 sheep is lost, Jesus would leave the 99 to find the one that is lost. That's how much he loves you. Just as sheep find shelter and protection under the shepherd, we will find the best protection and comfort under Jesus's guidance.

There is more! The story continues!

I left Tommy with a Bible and Christian books about the evidence of the Bible and why Christianity is the most reliable religion, and he was very thankful for it. However, one month later when I returned to Australia, I had two interesting dreams while taking a nap.

In the first dream, I was observing two big football teams playing against each other in a large football stadium. The final score was 2-5, but after the referee blew the final whistle, everyone was so thrilled, even though one team lost, yet the team that lost was celebrating as well as its fans. Then all the spectators went onto the football field and filled the football field with joy, laughter, and happiness, everyone celebrating together, not even one person was sad, and I did not understand why at all.

It was followed by another dream. In the dream, I was back at home in Myanmar and was standing beside the window in the living room on the 3rd floor of the residence, looking at the surroundings. Suddenly, I got a phone call from Tommy. Tommy, in a drunken voice, asked me "What is the zip code of your apartment number?" and "what is the zip code of the floor?" It is evident that he was too drunk to come to my home at that time.

I didn't understand the meaning or revelation of those two dreams clearly, and even though I prayed to God to give me the meaning of those dreams, I didn't get the understanding until the events happened. Then it was very clear to me. Tommy had been telling me that his Buddhist parents didn't like him reading the Christian books that I had given him as presents and they still didn't know he became a Christian. So his faith was shaking during those times, and I believe him being drunk in the dream was his faith being shaken outside by his parents as they kept telling him not to get influenced by books.

The next day, I slept just from 5:30 a.m. to 6:30 a.m. as I had class at 8 a.m. and even though I slept only 1 hour, I still had a dream of Tommy again. In the dream, I was in the basement of my home and Tommy was there with me! (He was trying to visit my home in the previous dream from the prior day). The basement was dimly lit with shelves all around the basement. And I pulled a container out of one of the shelves, and there were dirty 10cent gold color coins. I showed it to Tommy and was telling him "These are actually very valuable and are worth so much more than they look like" and then I woke up to my very annoying alarm ringing at 6: 30 a.m. I also didn't understand the meaning of my dream straightaway but told Tommy about the dream that day.

At college that day, I was reading my Bible and felt very moved by the verse as I dreamt of gold color coins that morning.

1 Peter 1:7 "These trials will show that your faith is genuine. It is being tested as fire tests and purifies gold, though your faith is far more precious than mere gold. So when your faith remains strong through many trials, it will bring you much praise and glory and honor on the day when Jesus Christ is revealed to the whole world."

I knew my faith was strong, but somehow I was feeling as if I had to save it for Tommy and I fell asleep at 9 p.m. that night which is extremely rare for me as I'm now even writing this at 2:37 a.m. Remember that I'm currently in Melbourne, Australia. Normally, I always sleep very late at night but that day, I was so tired and slept early, and I woke up to the noisy sound of the doorbell ringing at 1:30 in the morning! When I answered the call, there appeared a delivery man in the camera, and he said "Hello! This is the delivery for Lily!" In a very annoyed and sleepy voice, I said "You got the wrong address! There is no Lily here!" but he kept insisting that he had the right address, so I gave up and went to the ground floor to go tell him that he got the wrong address. When I got there and went outside the building, I just saw a car driving off, and there was completely nobody there at all, only me there alone. I even though like "maybe this is a trap that someone set up to rob me" but I trusted in Jesus that no evil would come near me. So as I was in a sleepy and annoyed state, I went back to my apartment and checked my phone notifications, and there were so many messages sent just 1 hour ago by Tommy, saying that he gave up on his faith, sounding very depressed.

It was like as if God made the delivery man mistakenly ring my doorbell so that I would wake up in time to text Tommy back to encourage him to keep his faith. Everything (when the bad things like the doorbell ringing at 1:30 a.m.!) was in perfect timing! I was surprised when I saw those messages and him declaring that he had given up on his faith in Jesus because of the persecution he suffered by every one of his relatives when his mum found him praying in his room. I went on explaining to him very carefully that his faith is so much more precious than he thinks and that he can still keep his faith in his heart and pray privately without making it evident to his family. Then it hit me when I remembered the dream and verse (1 Peter 1:7) that I had and saved for Tommy. God was preparing me for consoling him to keep his faith in Jesus all along! So I sent 1 Peter 1:7 to him, and he said he would keep his faith, what a relief.

So out of all the three dreams that I had(football, Tommy being drunk and me showing coins to Tommy), I only didn't still understand the 1st football dream where the score was 2-5, and everyone was celebrating wildly. I slept peacefully that night after consoling Tommy, and my mum called me in that morning when I woke up, saying that she got a necklace for me and was going to send it to me through my aunt who's coming to Melbourne. She then said my aunt is arriving at Melbourne on 25th (first mention of 2 and five since the dream) that month. My mum later told me that the necklace was the name of "Jesus"!

I was so happy as well as shocked as the football dream I had together with the dream of Tommy were connected all along, Jesus was only revealing to me that he had been with me all along since before I was even experiencing the situation on how to help Tommy keep his faith!

The next day, I had another dream of Tommy where he and I were sitting on the bus together traveling to a place. It is as God was showing me that he is back on track with his life. Because when he was an atheist, I also had a dream that we were driving a car on the highway to a destination but Tommy got off and was running in the opposite direction so happily. It was as if he was going the wrong way, but he didn't know, thinking that it's the right way. So I assumed he's back on track with his life now, which is amazing! He didn't talk with anyone else except me when he was very depressed after the unfortunate sudden death of his brother, and so when he got back on track, he had to restore the friendship he lost with some friends. He even sent me a screenshot where he texted a friend a very long message of apology saying "When MgMg took me out of my depression, I was saved by God and I felt it." Never in my life did I even think he would give credit about such thing to God which was an incredible testimony. And yes, my friends call me "Mg Mg" haha.

Now Tommy can even pray in other tongues (praying in the spirit), and his transformation from being a stubborn hardcore atheist who even declared to me that he wanted to spread atheism into being a devoted Christian who loves Jesus is truly amazing and also very unbelievable!

God is always out there for you!

Hebrews 13:5 "Never will I leave you; never will I forsake you."

He always answers

On one Sunday, I woke up late, was discouraged for some reasons and was lacking in faith in God. I even decided not to go to church anymore that day and texted Max "Sorry, I won't go to church today" as we usually always go to church together for the 6:30 p.m. service. I usually leave 30 minutes before the church service starts to get there in time and around 5:45 p.m., I was lying on the bed, thinking about life and the problems I had that time. Then I asked God "Father, please motivate me to go to church even though I am feeling so negative right now" and just some minutes later, Max called me saying "Hey! Where are you? I'm already at church! Come quick!" I was amazed as he was always late when going to church. I told him I was on my way. I thanked God for it! He later told me he didn't see my message at all (Thank God for that as well). Everyone was singing so passionately when I got to church, and I was looking at them raising their hands and singing, thinking to myself "How can they have such a strong faith? Why am I feeling negative today? Why do I feel like I'm losing faith today?" So I asked God about it.

After singing songs, the pastor said: ***"Faith comes by hearing and hearing the word of God"***(Romans 10:17 KJV), and it immediately answered what I asked God about. I realized that I had not been spending time reading the Bible or listening to Christian songs but more to watching movies and playing games and so, my faith was slowly dripping away throughout the week. And very surprisingly, Pastor "Steven Furtick" preached about Paul for the whole sermon from Philippians 1: 12-24. My bio caption on FaceBook happens to be that same Scripture quotation (Philippians 1: 21-24"). Such a coincidence! It was as if God was reaching out to me alone during the entire service.

Chapter 24

God's Encouragement

We can leave it to God

After I had written much of this book and sent it to my family by pdf through email, my parents were very happy to read it, and they made real physical books to share it with our relatives, but as some of our relatives couldn't read in English, they planned to translate it into the Burmese language.

After some weeks, they called me saying that they were going to contact a translation company and let them translate the book I've written and that it'll cost even about $100. However, I was a bit worried because the translator might not be a Christian so he wouldn't understand the book and might mistranslate some things (like the Bible verses or Christian terms). That night, I just trusted in God and told him it's out of my hands now to do anything about it and asked him to translate it in the best way possible. The next day early morning, my mum asked the chauffeur to drive to the translation company to translate the book, and so he went on his way. In the meantime, my mum went to my uncle's company and was talking about my book. While talking about my book, my uncle realized that he had a devoted Christian employee at his company and so he called the employee and asked about his suggestions for translating the book. Then he said a pastor at his church who also translates books from English to Burmese, had been working overseas but only came back a few days before and was going to meet her that Sunday (what perfect timing!). He kindly offered to give my book to her to translate it for free when he goes to church on Sunday. So when my mum called the chauffeur to ask if he had already paid the translation company $100 to translate the book and he said: "I'm almost there!" Such perfect timings! I have to believe the involvement of the hands of God is obvious here.

And so she asked him to kindly return the book so that they could give it to the employee of my uncle's company, who gave it to the pastor of his church to translate it. Then we could give it out to more relatives who could only read Burmese. My book has sparked an interest in Jesus for many people. My grandfather, who is in his 80's, said that throughout his life, he never knew the good side of Christianity.

Titus 2:11 *"For the grace of God has appeared that offers salvation to all people."*

Encouraged by God

So after having written most of this book, I was hesitant to share it with others as it contained personal stories. I was afraid that people would laugh at me, thinking that I am a very crazy religious freak. I imagined how people would look at me like I'm as one on the street with the signboard saying "YOU'RE GONNA BURN IN HELL" So one day after I finished writing most of my book at three o'clock in the morning, I was afraid to share it with anyone, so I prayed to God about it. Then before going to sleep, being so tired. I checked Instagram stories for a while and immediately saw a Christian page's story where they had three pictures.

The first picture said, "Do you have a story inside of you?"

The second picture said "Your story has the power to change someone's life.

Proverbs 18:21 *'Death and Life are in the power of the tongue (KJV)'"*

Then the third picture said, "Turn your story into a book that people will read."

I was so amazed at how God uses everything to guide us every day. It was posted only 1 hour ago which was amazing because that was the only time that I needed to see it. What's surprising is that the page usually posted Bible verses on their Instagram page. But, on that day, they were encouraging people to write a book about their stories.

So I took it as a sign from God encouraging me to write this book to save lost people and change their minds from having an evil twisted negative view of God into understanding that God is the opposite of what they thought. That God is loving and caring God.

God Never Disappoints!

So as a young child, did I ever think of becoming an author? Never and by never, I mean, not even one time! I just wanted God to use me to reach out to so many people out there, and so I wrote this book and God has helped me with everything in this process. I did not know anything about how the Book publishing area worked at all as I had no interest in it and never even once inquired about it in my life before I wrote this book.

Did I write this book, knowing that by now, it would be in your hands? Absolutely not because who am I? That was the question I struggled to answer. Who am I that I would even be able to write and publish a book with an amazing Christian Book Publishing Company that would spread this book to so many people around the world. It was so much more than I ever imagined.

I am just an ordinary 18 years old college student who wrote a book to share with people I met about Jesus. I have no qualifications and no previous publications to have a chance to find a Publisher for myself.

Please let me share with you how the journey was for me in producing this book.

When I was in the middle process of writing this book, I had a friend from college whose father is a Pastor, and he told me that 'maybe' his dad could publish my book for me when I'm done. Out of excitement, when I finished writing a shorter version of this book, I said to him "Hey I'm done, please ask your dad for me." He said, "yea sure, but I cannot guarantee anything." I waited and waited and never heard from him again for the publication of my book. At least, a reply with a "No, I'm sorry" would have been appreciated. However, I have realized that it was all part of God's plan for my book to be distributed to so many people around the world. So, I was a little disappointed. I did not know whom to go to or whom to ask. I asked God to let me feel the prompting of the spirit inside me to know if I should ask the pastors at Church but I did not feel anything when I was near them. Now, you can imagine how I was thinking. I was an 18-year-old college student wanting his book to get published.

As time passed by, I had more things to write about, and so I wrote them and tried my best to desperately ask for help from anybody that seemed that they could help me. I emailed my book to some Pastors and people telling them "it's the book about my testimony and my life with God. I want to publish this book. Can you please recommend a book publishers that I can contact for my book to get published? If you don't know, can you please kindly suggest me whom I can contact to ask help for connections?" I waited and waited, and I got no reply. Of course, I felt very disappointed and even asked God if he wanted me to share this book anymore. I did not understand anything, but I trusted God to open a door for me and kept on trying. Getting no help from anyone was also part of God's plan. God was closing doors that were not good for me.

So one day, I just searched on the internet randomly about finding book publishers for a Christian book. Then I found a website that Authors had to submit their sample manuscript and the publishers check it and contact the authors when they're interested. However, it was costly, and I did not have enough pocket-money to try for it. So I just talked to God "Father, if you want me to use this website, please provide for me and make it obvious." A week passed by and my parents unexpectedly gave me pocket-money which was the exact same amount that was required to submit the sample manuscript in the website. So by faith, I trusted that God wanted me to use it and I paid and used it, and the rest is history as you know.

Of course, I was worried that no book publishers would even contact me as I had no qualifications or even any previous publications to show off that would impress them to be interested in publishing my book. I was a nobody and was the least likely to be chosen among anybody there. However, I had complete faith in God that he would find me the right book publisher that would distribute my book around the world. When Advbooks contacted me saying they're interested in publishing my book, I could not even believe it as I thought it was just an imaginary dream that I had. But God is faithful, and he will always provide for us. That's when I knew the answer to who am I that I would even get my book distributed to so many people around the world. **I am a child of God.**

If God can do this for me, God can do anything for you I am sure! He'll give you the desires of your heart if you delight in him. God has so much more in store for us than we can ever imagine.

Psalm 139:17-18 (NLT) "How precious are your thoughts about me, O God. They cannot be numbered! I can't even count them; they outnumber the grains of sand! And when I wake up, you are still with me!"

Romans 5:8(NLT) "But God showed his great love for us by sending Christ to die for us while we were still sinners."

You are loved more than you will ever know by someone who died to know you

Romans 8:38(NLT) "And I am convinced that nothing can ever separate us from God's love. Neither death nor life, neither angels or demons, neither our fears for today nor our worries about tomorrow — not even the powers of hell can separate us from God's love."

Ephesians 3:20(NLT) "Now all glory to God, who is able, through his mighty power at work within us, to accomplish infinitely more than we might ask or think."

Ephesians 3:19(NLT) "May you experience the love of Christ, though it is too great to understand fully. Then you will be made complete with the fullness of life and power that comes from God."

How great is our God!

Below is the Father's Love Letter that I mentioned earlier in my book. Open your heart and let God speak to you directly through his words in the Bible.

My Child,

You may not know me, but I know everything about you (Psalm 139:1) I know when you sit down and when you rise up. (Psalm 139:2). I am familiar with all your ways (Psalm 139:3). Even the very hairs on your head are numbered. Matthew 10:29-31 For you were made in my image (Genesis 1:27). In me you live and move and have your being (Acts

17:28). For you are my offspring (Acts 17:28) I knew you even before you were conceived (Jeremiah 1:4-5). I chose you when I planned creation (Ephesians 1:11-12). You were not a mistake, for all your days are written in my book (Psalm 139:15-16). I determined the exact time of your birth and where you would live (Acts 17:26). You are fearfully and wonderfully made (Psalm 139:14). I knit you together in your mother's womb (Psalm 139:13). And brought you forth on the day you were born (Psalm 71:6).

I have been misrepresented by those who don't know me. (John 8:41-44). I am not distant and angry but am the complete expression of love. (1 John 4:16). And it is my desire to lavish my love on you (1 John 3:1). Simply because you are my child and I am your Father (1 John 3:1). I offer you more than your earthly father ever could (Matthew 7:11) For I am the perfect father (Matthew 5:48). Every good gift that you receive comes from my hand (James 1:17). For I am your provider and I meet all your needs (Matthew 6:31-33). My plan for your future has always been filled with hope (Jeremiah 29:11). Because I love you with an everlasting love. (Jeremiah 31:3). My thoughts toward you are countless as the sand on the seashore (Psalm 139:17-18). And I rejoice over you with singing (Zephaniah 3:17). I will never stop doing good to you (Jeremiah 32:40). For you are my treasured possession (Exodus 19:5).

I desire to establish you with all my heart and all my soul (Jeremiah 32:41). And I want to show you great and marvelous things (Jeremiah 33:3). If you seek me with all your heart, you will find me (Deuteronomy 4:29). Delight in me and I will give you the desires of your heart (Psalm 37:4). For it is I who gave you those desires (Philippians 2:13).

I am able to do more for you than you could possibly imagine (Ephesians 3:20). For I am your greatest encourager (2 Thessalonians 2:16-17). I am also the Father who comforts you in all your troubles (2 Corinthians 1:3-4). When you are brokenhearted, I am close to you (Psalm 34:18). As a shepherd carries a lamb, I have carried you close to my heart (Isaiah 40:11). One day I will wipe away every tear from your eyes (Revelation 21:3-4). And I'll take away all the pain you have suffered on this earth (Revelation 21:3-4).

I am your Father, and I love you even as I love my son, Jesus (John 17:23). For in Jesus, my love for you is revealed (John 17:26). He is the exact representation of my being (Hebrews 1:3). He came to demonstrate that I am for you, not against you (Romans 8:31). And to tell you that I am not counting your sins (2 Corinthians 5:18-19). Jesus died so that you and I could be reconciled (2 Corinthians 5:18-19). His death was the ultimate expression of my love for you (1 John 4:10). I gave up everything I loved that I might gain your love (Romans 8:31-32).

If you receive the gift of my son Jesus, you receive me (1 John 2:23). And nothing will ever separate you from my love again (Romans 8:38-39). Come home, and I'll throw the biggest party heaven has ever seen (Luke 15:7). I have always been Father, and will always be Father (Ephesians 3:14-15). My question is… Will you be my child? (John 1:12-13). I am waiting for you (Luke 15:11-32).

Love, Your Dad
(Almighty God).

Chapter 25

From Me to You

Now, most of you may think that Christian people are just trying to force or make people become Christians by telling them constantly non-stop about Christianity. You may think they just want to save you from Hell out of their imagination or that their main intention is to make Christianity a dominating religion out of all other religions.

This is not true at all because we're only doing this so that people would experience the love of God for them and have a close relationship with the one who loves us unconditionally that he even gave up his only son for us so that we may have a relationship with him. His love for us is relentless and unconditional.

You may ask "How can anyone ever take away the sins of another person? It's impossible! That sinful person has to suffer for their own mistakes! That is karma!"

Please let me explain you with a simple analogy. Imagine a 40 years old father and his seven years old son walk into a shop, just admiring the sculptures of artwork available there. Suddenly, the son accidentally knocks down a $500 vase, and it broke into little pieces. And the seven-year-old son has no job or any ways of getting money to have enough money to pay for the damage he caused in the store. So who pays for it? Clearly, the father! He would do that because of his love for his own son. Even if the son broke a 1 million dollars vase and the father doesn't have enough money to pay for the damage, he would go to jail for his son instead of sending his son to prison. It's out of fatherly love.

This is just like God and us. We sinned against a Holy God, and he died for us, out of pure Fatherly love so that we may not die eternally.

Here's another example based on a true story. A 17 years old girl was arrested for driving a car over the speed limit. In court, she was charged with $250,000 for other crimes she committed in the past. She had no job and no money at all to pay for it. Then miraculously, the Judge who charged her $250,000, paid the whole amount for her and let her go. Everyone was astonished. Later, it was found out that the Judge was her father! It's once again, just like God and us, God paid the punishment for us, we only have to accept the payment which was made by Jesus on the cross, just as the 17 years old girl did for her crimes in the story. She could have rejected it and gone to jail, but she accepted it. God never pushes or forces us, but he always gives us a free choice to accept or reject the payment he made for us because that is love. Love always gives a free choice. Just as you see in movies or cartoons, the kind-hearted character never forces the girl he likes to love him back, but he gives her a free choice to reject or accept him. God loves us so much! Jesus died for you out of love, knowing that you might even use his name as a curse word.

Now many people question Christianity as dangerous. They assume Christians would have a mindset that they are free to do whatever they want, knowing that they are forgiven of their sins. They really are free to do whatever they want as their sins are forgiven, but they choose not to do it as their hearts have been changed inside out! How? Let me explain it to you by a simple analogy.

Imagine a 20-year-old criminal who regrets the crimes he committed both "unintentionally" and "intentionally" in the past is captured and is in custody, being told he would be in Jail the next day, for so many years. That night in custody, he would be extremely disappointed and depressed, regretting everything he did in the past. The next day when he was about to be thrown into prison, he found out that someone who knows everything about him paid the price for his release! When he meets that person, he would be so incredibly grateful and would want to serve and be with that person his whole life. So his heart is changed inside out, and his life is transformed, he would no longer commit any more crimes as he would want to honor the one who saved him from prison time. His heart and life are changed! This is just like Jesus with us! Jesus even said: the one who is forgiven more loves more. If the criminal had a 1-month prison sentence and was released by the man, he wouldn't love him as much as if he was released from a life sentence in prison. And when we think about it, we all have our own very dark sins that we have never told anyone.

150

Jesus came here not to be served but to serve, laying his life down for all of our sins so that we have eternal life by believing in him.

Now if you're an atheist or an agnostic, you may have some Christian friends trying to persuade you to come to church. Please just read this analogy that would describe why they are doing it to you.

Imagine you're with your family, relatives and friends in the desert and water is very limited among your group. One day, you wanted to explore so you wondered off afar and found a river! The river contains magically very clean water with fishes in it. So you drink from it, catch fishes and eat it until you're fully satisfied. You become very healthy in just a day.

Then when you have enough strength to travel back to your family and friends, you would even run to them to tell them about the good news of the river. You would tell them about how there's an abundance for things you need and how good life is there. You would want to convince them to come to the river with you. That's precisely the same situation that I am in right now, being the only devoted Christian in a Buddhist family, relatives, and friends.

So when they ask you for proof of the river, you can show them your full and satisfied stomach, how you even have enough energy to run around them or even show them the tiny pieces of fish meat left on your lips. Those things are the things that were from the river (proof of God's grace in your life; example like you becoming a peaceful person when you were short tempered before or just of experiences of God's protection/guidance in your life).

People see the evidence with their own eyes, but some are very stubborn or ignorant of the truth. They reject that the river is really there by thinking of every other possible ways of you having tiny pieces of fish meat on your lips. Those are the type of people that will still even doubt you if you bring a whole fish to them in the desert, saying that it's from the river. They would think the fish just fell from the sky. They need to be open-minded and take a leap of faith to experience heaven on Earth and not reject the Holy Spirit trying to enter into their lives.

You're crying your heart out, saying so desperately "Please trust me! The river is really there. Just come along with me, and you'll see for yourself. Please" but then they respond that "You may just have been hallucinating, we don't trust you. A river in the desert? Are you crazy? No, we won't go to see the river that you're talking about. It surely is not there."

It's unfortunate and heartbreaking when you know the truth, and everyone rejects it. Take this book as a whole fish from the river and trust me, please. I already gave you so much information about how real and loving God is and has been throughout my life.

Faith is taking the first step even when you don't see the whole staircase

Everything we do is by faith. Even the chairs we are sitting on are by faith. We don't pick it up and see if it would hold our weight. By faith, we sit down on it, assured that people would not build a chair that wouldn't hold our weight.

Just put that same small faith in Jesus Christ, and you will know who Jesus is. You accept him by 'faith,' and he comes into your heart and life. Then you will finally know that he is who he claims to be (Billy Graham, Chicago, 1971, sermon: Who is Jesus?)

> *Deuteronomy 4:29 "If you seek me with all your heart, you will find me."*

You may be thinking if you're not good enough to have a relationship with God yet. Well, just as you don't clean yourself before taking a shower, come to God just as you are no matter how dirty or in a messed up situation you are and he will clean you inside out.

God can change your heart if you let him! He will change it "inside out" not "outside in."

Inside out is when you are changed from the inside, and the result comes out. It becomes very obvious when you become patient when in the past, you were easily angry or becoming more loving and caring towards others even though in the past you had a cold heart and wanted to be all alone by yourself. You don't need to control yourself; you will become patient and loving! Instead of 'trying' to become patient and loving! Instead of hatred towards a person who did you wrong, you'll only have love for him/her and will want to change his heart into becoming like yours! You'll have a heart like Jesus once you truly know how much he went through on the Cross for people who hated him, knowing that they might never love him back. That is pure love.

Outside in is when you try to control your actions outside yourself by controlling your mind such as doing meditation and squeezing in every ounce of anger you have inside instead of letting it out when the situation comes. This is bad for health and psychological issues too. By this way, one tries to become patient. He tries to change his heart by controlling his mind whereas in the inside out method, one 'becomes' patient instead of trying to be!

It's your choice to choose whichever method you like for your future!

Here's a simple and easy prayer if you want to accept Jesus as your lord and savior, turn away from all your sins in the past no matter how bad it might have been and have a brand new life and relationship with God. Your life will never be the same after you've said this prayer with your mouth and especially with all your heart.

"Father God, I repent. Forgive me of all my sins. I confess with my mouth that Jesus is my lord and savior. I believe that you raised him from the dead. So I ask you to please come into my heart, live your life for me and end the old me. From this moment on, I am yours. Thank you for saving me and accepting me into your family. In Jesus' name, Amen."

Romans 10:9 "If you declare with your mouth, 'Jesus is Lord,' and believe in your heart that God raised him from the dead, you will be saved."

Congratulations if you've said that prayer! All I've written would be all worth it even if one person gets saved. The next steps for you would be to start reading the Bible, join a local church and immerse yourself into Christian behavior! Remember that you can cast all your worries and troubles on the lord and he will solve all the problems that you have.

If you've made it this far, I thank you so much for taking your time to read about how God has helped me through my life's tough situations. I am sure you'll also experience miracles and breakthroughs in your life when you depend on God for it and have a close relationship with him every day. May God bless you always!

Acknowledgements

This book has only been made possible because of God and all the amazing people that believed in me and supported me even though I was just a Nobody.

To my parents: You both are the best parents I could ever have! No wonder God gave me such Parents who really believes in my potential, loves me and sacrificed so much for me. This gave me the courage to complete writing my book. I really could never have done it without your support. I will never be able to thank you enough for everything you have done for me.

To my sister: Even though you are really annoying sometimes, I thank you so much for being the most encouraging person to me in writing this book. It was because of you that I continued writing so much more after writing just a little bit which made all this possible. Thank you so much for believing in my potential and being an amazing sister to me!

To Hillsong Church: Thank you everyone for making me feel so welcomed just as I were at home every time I enter. The Community that I have from church really encouraged me so much and helped me keep my faith strong as the only devoted Christian friends I have is mostly from Hillsong Church. They are the ones I can share my problems with and help me grow in knowledge and faith. Thank you to the volunteer team for helping me grow in my uncomfortable areas and making me a much better person for ministry.

To Ashley Mozhuman: I thank God so much that I met an amazing Volunteer group leader like you. You are really an amazing godly leader. It was also because of your encouragement that I dared to submit my sample manuscript on the manuscript submission website which led me to meeting the Advantage Books team. Your encouraging words gave me spiritual power inside and motivated me even more to write the rest of the book in style. Thank you so much for everything. I am looking forward to serving more services with you and bringing more people to faith together at Hillsong Church, by God's grace.

To Heather Cetrangolo: I am so very blessed to have you as my mentor whom I can go to anytime I have any questions about anything in the Bible. I really believe that without you, I would not grow in my knowledge and faith as much as I am supposed to. I am very honored to be part of the Chapel's House Party team. I am looking forward to learning more from you and saving more people together in the future!, by God's grace. Thank you so much for everything!

To Grace Baldwin: Thank you so much for everything, my perfect girlfriend. I'm really so blessed to have you in my life. I am so excited to go through this amazing life together with you, guided by God in every steps of our lives as we simply keep on walking together on the path that He has laid out for us with his perfect love and grace. I love you so much.

To the Advantage Books team: It's such a blessing to work together with you! Thank you for giving me the chance to publish my book and share my story with so many people around the world. That was the prayer I had been praying for and you are the answer to my prayer just 4 days after praying for my manuscript to be found by an amazing Christian Book Publishing Company. I never even thought this would be possible for me at all. Thank you so much for your kind patience in working together with me.

I know God has put everyone that I had met in my life for me to strengthen me, encourage me and push me forward in my life. Without one of those people that I mentioned, I really would lack something in finishing writing my book. I am so thankful to God for putting all of you in my life for me.

To my Lord and Savior, Jesus Christ: You have given me so much more than I could even ask for or imagined. Your love and grace is so amazing. I will live every day of my life for you only and one day, preach to so many lost people out there about the good news of the Gospel for you, by your grace towards me. I know I don't have that ability and am weak in that area now, but where I'm weak, you're strong. I will live out my life for you and can't wait to see you face to face in the future in a place where evil does not exist anymore.

To you: It's such a blessing for me that you've taken time to read my book. I thank you so much for your time. I really pray and hope that you'll be able to grow in your knowledge and relationship with God deeper than before. God has so much more in store for you than you can ever imagine.

I know it's hard to believe it first but if God can do this for me, God can do anything for you! Remember that I am no better than you. You are qualified for an abundance of blessings by Jesus' death on the cross out of love for you, not by your works. God bless you and may he take you into the unknown, equip you with what you need and make you a living testimony of how amazing God is, through you to other people, in Jesus' name, Amen.

Bibliography

Books

Andrew Newberg and Mark Robert Waldman, "Born to Believe", 2006, Atria Books.

Medley, B. (2013). Religion is For Fools. 2nd ed. Authentic Media Inc., pg.21, 23, 26, 27, 32.

Mark Virkler and Patti Virkler, "How to hear God's voice", 2006, Destiny Image Publishers, pg. 200, 201

Strobel, L. (2016). The Case for Christ: A Journalist's Personal Investigation of the Evidence for Jesus. Zondervan, p.33.

Film

Creation Seminar 1 – Kent Hovind – Age of the Earth (2005). [DVD] Directed by K. Hovind.

Creation Seminar 3 - Kent Hovind – Dinosaurs and the Bible. (2005). [DVD] Directed by K. Hovind.

Patterns of Evidence: Exodus. (2014). [DVD] Directed by T. Mahoney. United States: Thinking Man Films.

100 Reasons why Evolution is stupid (Video documentary)-Kent Hovind (2001).

Journals

Baumgardner, J. R., et al., Measurable 14C in fossilized organic materials: confirming the young earth creation-flood model, Proceedings of the Fifth International Conference on Creationism, vol. II, Creation Science Fellowship (2003), Pittsburgh, PA, pg.127-142. Archived at www.icr.org/i/pdf/research/RATE_ICC_Baum gardner.pdf.

Nathaniel T Jeanson, "A Young Earth Creation Human Mitochondrial DNA "Clock": Whole Mitochondrial Mutation Rate Confirms D-Loop Results, "Answers Research Journal 8 (2015): 375-378.

Nicole Arce, "Massive Genetic Study Reveals 90 Percent of Earth's Animals Appeared At The Same Time" Tech Times, 2018.

Scoville, Heather. "Nebraska Man." ThoughtCo, Mar. 30, 2016, thoughtco.com/nebraska-man-1224737.

SMITHSONIAN ADMITS TO DESTRUCTION OF THOUSANDS OF GIANT HUMAN SKELETONS IN EARLY 1900's, World News Daily Report, 2017.

Articles

Mark Virkler, "Health Benefits of Speaking in Tongues", 2014.

Hillsong Music Credits

For more information contact:

Maung Maung Kyaw Zaw Hein
C/O Advantage Books
PO Box 160847
Altamonte Springs, FL 32779

info@advbooks.com

To purchase additional copies of this book visit our bookstore website at:
www.advbookstore.com

PO Box 160847
Altamonte Springs, FL 32779

Longwood, Florida, USA
"we bring dreams to life"™
www.advbookstore.com

Made in the USA
Las Vegas, NV
22 March 2023

69504205R00089